THE REFRACTIVE THINKER

AN ANTHOLOGY OF HIGHER LEARNING

Volume Four:
Ethics, Leadership, and Globalization

Edited by
Dr. Cheryl A. Lentz

The Refractive Thinker™ Press

The Refractive Thinker: An Anthology of Higher Learning
Volume IV: Ethics, Leadership, and Globalization

The Refractive Thinker™ Press
9065 Big Plantation Avenue
Las Vegas, NV 89143-5440   USA

Orders@lentzleadership.com
Websites: www.lentzleadership.com
                   www.refractivethinker.com

Books are available through The Refractive Thinker™ Press at special discounts for bulk purchases for the purpose of sales promotion, seminar attendance, or educational purposes. Special volumes can be created for specific purposes and to organizational specifications. Please contact us for further details.

Library of Congress Control Number: 2010903601

Volume ISBNs
   Soft Cover   978-0-9823036-8-9
   E-book/PDF   978-0-9823036-9-6
   Kindle version available.

Refractive Thinker™ logo by Joey Root, The Refractive Thinker™ Press logo and cover design by Jacqueline Teng, final production by Gary A. Rosenberg.

Printed in the United States of America

10   9   8   7   6   5   4   3   2   1

Contents

Foreword, vii

Preface, ix

Acknowledgements, xi

What lies behind us and what lies before us
are tiny matters compared to
what lies within us.

—RALPH WALDO EMERSON

Foreword

This collection of new articles about ethical leadership in a global context provides insights from scholars that is as important to the practitioner's world as it is to students and academics. In a world where Enron, WorldCom, and AIG have created cynicism about the integrity of the modern organization, the need to focus on the ethical duties of leaders and organizations is more important today than at any time in the last century.

The insights of these scholars offers a perspective about ethical duties that enables leaders to examine their day-to-day actions, claims about commitment to ideals, and the underlying assumptions that form the basis of true beliefs. This self-examination process is critical as we reflect on the integrity of organizations, the creation of trust, and the obligations of those who lead.

Leadership must be ethical if leaders are to pursue the active participation and cooperation of others. Only when leaders serve with integrity will they earn the followership of others. Leaders must become the personification of the ideals that they proclaim and become the benefactors of others in a world mired in self-interest.

Leaders have the moral obligation to challenge the thinking of those with whom they live and work, asking others to honor obligations to society in a way that creates value and sustains the future.

The leader-follower relationship adds value only when leaders are trustworthy and act with a commitment to the welfare, growth, and wholeness of society and those whom they serve.

This volume provides the reader with the opportunity to examine ideas about leadership, the standards by which we must govern, and the obligations that we owe to others within a world that is facing constant moral pressures to compromise our values in the pursuit of self-interest. The message of this volume is that we must willingly examine the underlying foundations of our thinking as we reflect on the opportunities and duties that confront us.

Leadership is far more than an exchange relationship or a simple quid pro quo transaction. The leader's obligation requires the leader to help an organization to become its best, but along the way the leader must also demonstrate a transformational commitment to employees, customers, and others served by the organization.

As stewards in a world that is struggling to survive, leaders owe others a profound set of covenantal responsibilities. Leaders must not only be the servants of others, but they must also teach correct principles so that others may govern themselves. Leaders not only inspire others but they build partnerships with others in the discovery and creation of new meanings and profound new truths about life and about organizational work.

The message of this volume is that we have much to learn about leadership; about ethical duty; and about a world that has become smaller, more interrelated, and more difficult to define. Although the authors of this volume do not profess to possess all of the answers about the topics addressed herein, their insights offer opportunities for discussion about principles that affect each one of us—both today and in the years ahead.

—Cam Caldwell, PhD

Preface

I *think* therefore I am.
—RENÉ DESCARTES

I *critically think* to be.
I *refractively think* to change the world.

Welcome to *The Refractive Thinker: Volume IV:*
Ethics, Leadership, and Globalization.

Thank you for joining us for the first 2010 edition, Volume IV, as we continue to celebrate the accomplishments of these doctoral scholars affiliated with many phenomenal institutions of higher learning. The purpose of this next offering in the anthology series is to share yet another glimpse into the scholarly works of these authors, specifically on the topics of ethics, leadership, and concerns within the global landscape of business.

In addition to exploring various aspects of ethics and globalization, the purpose of *The Refractive Thinker*™ is also to serve the tenets of leadership. Leadership is not simply a concept outside of the self, but comes from within, defining our very essence; where the search to define leadership becomes our personal journey not yet a finite destination. In the words of Dr. Thomas Woodruff (2009) "Change has no conclusion" (RT: Vol. III, p. 213).

The Refractive Thinker™ is an intimate expression of who we are—the ability to think beyond the traditional boundaries of thinking and critical thinking. Instead of mere reflection and evaluation, one challenges the very boundaries of the constructs itself. If thinking is *inside* the box, and critical thinking is *outside* the box, we add the next step of refractive thinking, *beyond* the box. As in our first three volumes, the authors within these pages are on a mission to change the world, never satisfied or quite content with what is or asking *why*, instead these authors intentionally strive to push and test the limits to ask *why not*. Join us on this next adventure of *The Refractive Thinker*™ where Volume IV continues the discussion specifically themed to explore the realm of ethics, leadership, and globalization. This offers yet another bite of the apple from the tree of knowledge upon an ever expanding canvas from which these authors choose to cast their paint, envisioning new horizons in which to move forward and explore the future.

I invite you to join with me as we venture forward to showcase these authors of Volume IV. The goal is to offer a chance to bring to publication more ideas for which the audience may be interested in the expertise and guidance that they offer.

Please contact The Refractive Thinker Press for further information regarding these authors and the works contained within these pages. Perhaps you or your organization may be looking for their expertise to incorporate as part of your annual corporate meetings as a key note or guest speaker (s), perhaps to offer individual or group seminars or coaching, or require their expertise as consultants.

We look forward to your interest in discussing future opportunities. Let this continue our journey begun with volume I to which *The Refractive Thinker*™ will serve as our guide to this and future volumes. Come join us in our quest to be refractive thinkers and add your wisdom to the collective. We look forward to your stories.

Acknowledgments

The foundation of leadership embraces the art of asking questions—to validate and affirm what we do and why. Leaders often challenge this status quo, to offer alternatives and new directions, to dare to try something that has not yet been done as again proved true in this case with volume IV. This publication required the continued leap of faith and belief in this new publishing model by those willing to continue forward on this voyage. As a result, please let me express my gratitude for the help of the many that made this project possible.

First, let me offer a special thank you to Trish Hladek, my husband Bill Lentz, and Dr. Tom Woodruff and his wife Diane for their unwavering support and belief that traversing unchartered waters is worthy of the journey. My gratitude extends to our Peer Review Board to include: Dr. Tom Woodruff, Dr. Laura Grandgenett, and Dr. Michael Elia; and our Board of Directors to include: Dr. Elmer Hall, Dr. Edward Knab, Dr. Judy Blando, Dr. Lisa Kangas, Dr. Tom Woodruff, (and myself); as well as our production specialist, Gary Rosenberg; Refractive Thinker logo designer, Joey Root; and cover and companion website designer, Jacqueline Teng.

Let me also extend my sincere thanks to all the participating authors who continue to believe in this project as we move forward with our eyes to the future. We appreciate their commitment to leadership, and to the concept of what it means to be a Refractive Thinker™.

Dr. Cheryl A. Lentz
Managing Editor
Las Vegas, NV
April 2010

CHAPTER 1

Ethics in Educational Leadership

Dr. Neysa T. Sensenig

E ducational leadership requires an educator to make substantive decisions that affect staff, students, and community. Good sound judgment and practical implementation support the social and economic influences that these decisions have on a school community. To accomplish this endeavor, an educational leader needs a personal ethical belief to support moral decision-making. Therefore, this chapter proposes educational leaders develop an understanding of ethical theory to form an ethical belief leading to sound judgments based upon personal, moral deliberation exemplifying best practices to facilitate good educational decision-making.

A REVIEW OF ETHICAL STUDY

In this first section, the philosophical theories of Plato, Aristotle, Immanuel Kant, and John Stuart Mill provide an ethical foundation for educational leadership. Ethical thought secures a foundation in ancient writings as early philosophers attempted to make sense of society and interpersonal relationships. The study of ethics is the "study of ideas, ideas about right and wrong" (Beckner, 2004, p. 25). Philosophers perpetuated the study of ethics as civilizations developed and matured into large nations and powers. The resolution of societal dilemmas is important to achieving happiness and the good life through "a more orderly, more thoughtful approach to solving problems" (Beckner, p. 48). The philosophical theories of Plato, Aristotle, Immanuel Kant, and John Stuart Mill provide a diverse foundation of ethical thought for educational leaders when looking for the best solution to solve difficult problems and carryout leadership responsibilities.

Theory of Morality

The early philosophical writings of Plato established a moral foundation for further development of ethical thought and action based on virtue. Plato emphasized a social order specifying a place for each person within society and a system for fulfilling personal obligations. However, he pursued a universal truth supporting the worthwhile endeavors of others in the public arena (Vassallo, 2004). In Plato's view, an individual's motivation for action is the virtue to do what is right as expressed by those select few who consider the whole society (Beckner, 2004). Plato referred to virtue as not innate; however, a person can be assisted by thinkers in recollecting what was known before the present life began (Klugman & Stump, 2006). Plato's moral theory focused upon *the what and the how* of philosophical questions (Vassallo). Answers were not important, only the aspect of questioning (Vassallo).

Theory of Value and Virtue

In contrast, Aristotle focused more on the subject matter and his opinion of the subject (Beckner, 2004). Aristotle established values and virtues to assist the individual in making correct ethical choices; happiness guides an individual to two types of virtue: moral and intellectual (Vassallo, 2004). One achieved virtuousness through contemplation and calculation of issues and made the right choices by developing a value system (Beckner; Vassallo). This value system provided a person with the tools, or virtues, to discover the right action in the right situation somewhere between two possible variables (Beckner; Klugman & Stump, 2006). The individual then used the multiple disciplines of art, science, prudence, wisdom, and intuition to find the various avenues for seeking Truth (Vassallo). Educational leaders must develop value systems to support individuals to make correct ethical choices regarding behavior.

Theory of Moral Objectivism

Moral objectivists followed principles or rules that serve good reason as the best guidance in making practical decisions (Beckner, 2004). Immanuel Kant professed either divine law or natural law as the basic principle for guidance in acting ethically. However, natural inclinations must be subjugated to a law that was "universally binding on all rational beings" (Beckner, p. 53). Kant used the term categorical imperative to explain the universal maxims that one can reach through powers of reason by weighing principles against other moral principles (Beckner). This categorical imperative applied to all and denoted decision-making that applied to all. The 'principle of ends' referred to individual actions to treat all humanity as an end and not as a means to the end (Beckner). In educational settings, rules and laws guide all individuals to act according to the universal principles of the institution.

Theory of Utilitarianism

In the development of ethical study, the relativist theory followed utilitarianism to promote actions proportionally right to achieve happiness; that is, the greatest good for the greatest number (Patterson, 2005). Philosophers of the time associated utilitarianism with social Darwinism and the survival of the fittest. However, J. S. Mill did not make this connection between utilitarianism and social Darwinism because Mill rejected nature as an ethical model and placed "emphasis on human social and personal development" (Patterson, p. 74). Mill stated pleasure was the highest moral principle, albeit not a selfish or self-centered principle, but an aggregate happiness for all (Patterson). The measures of happiness were impartial with much regard for the happiness of others as for one's self (Beckner, 2004; Patterson). When making ethical decisions, leaders should consider the pleasure and pain of others; and wise leaders make the best decision. The moral and intellectual development of people is important to produce a society of happy and ethical people (Beckner; Patterson). The emphasis upon individual equity is important to the relativist as Mill wrote women failed to reach full potential because they did not have equal educational opportunities (Patterson). Consequently, Mill believed women who advanced toward happiness would have a positive effect on the character of men (Patterson).

Recommendation: Ethical Study

Ethical study should provide educational leaders with the ability to develop reasoning skills to make up their own minds (Klugman & Stump, 2006). Leaders should resist following ethical teachings as one set of morals or values established as the one best ethically correct behavior. Leaders need to evaluate and reason what is best culturally in an ethically diverse setting of educational institutions (Klugman & Stump). Through an understanding of ethical thought, leaders can change core values and beliefs to increase moral reasoning ability when making decisions requiring analytical problem solving and various outcomes (Klugman & Stump). Lyndale (as stated in

Klugman & Stump) reflected that understanding ethical theory supports critical thinking skills and allows one to participate in evaluating decision-making and developing moral reasoning skills. The next section recommends a practical approach to educational leaders in developing a personal ethical belief.

ON DEVELOPING A PERSONAL ETHICAL BELIEF

The ethical theories of Plato, Aristotle, Kant, and Mill espoused perspectives an educational leader can legitimately use to act ethically within the educational environment. In addition to an understanding of ethical theory, an educational leader needs a sound personal ethical belief for moral decisions. Three sound approaches to developing a personal ethical belief include rules-based thinking (deontology), ends-based thinking (teleology), and care-based thinking (value theory) (Kidder, 1995 as in Beckner, 2004).

Theory of Deontology

One theoretical perspective of ethical belief is the objective basis of duty to a higher organization like church, family, or society. Thus, deontology theory judges action on whether an action is right or wrong without individual interpretation (Beckner, 2004). Individual principles should benefit the society based on common needs to maintain continuity and stability in society (Beckner). Rules provide a system by which one can act morally without thinking about day-to-day actions.

The difficulty with deontology as the only ethical belief system is the stagnant state of affairs when personal action occurs through rote, unchanging, or universal behavior (Beckner, 2004). Human response becomes entrenched in an action based on a one-way-based rule system of an earlier society. The acceptance of a one basic set of principles can create difficulty when one basic rule comes in conflict with another basic rule (Beckner). No mechanism for handling stark contrasts in conflict exists, and the only method for change would be revolution. The educational leader should consider end-based thinking, or teleology, as a second ethical belief system when developing best practices in educational decision-making.

Theory of Teleology

Beckner (2004) said a consequentialist approach to ethical thought reflects an assessment of consequences and a forecasting of outcomes as the primary mechanism for action. The theory of teleology seeks to control an action through deterrent or preventive measures based upon consequences. Self-interest, for the teleologist, promotes social good because pleasing the self, leads to supporting society. This view of teleology is similar to the theory of egoism, which urges everyone to seek the good life so long-term interests will succeed over short-term interests (Beckner). The concept of utilitarianism is similar to the theory of teleology as utilitarianism includes consequentialism and the utility principle. Each individual seeks pleasure and an acceptance of individual action based on the extent that the individual derives pleasure, does not derive pleasure, or experiences pain (Beckner).

Because society cannot identify what is acceptable or universally 'good' behavior, teleology helps one avoid the total acceptance of following rules that deontology requires (Beckner, 2004). Teleology does not identify who will determine what is right or wrong rather teleology protects innocent people from being taken advantage of unfairly or treated inappropriately (Beckner). Beckner says those who fail to act appropriately are punished accordingly and "the punishment should fit the crime" (p. 66). For the educational leader, the ethical beliefs of deontology and teleology resolve some basic ethical dilemmas while leaving other dilemmas unresolved. Another ethical belief system for the educational leader to use in decision-making is value theory.

Value Theory

The ethicist who focuses on value theory incorporates some aspects of deontology and teleology in the description of a good person and how this good person develops (Beckner, 2004). A person who believes in a value system identifies the priorities in valuing the good life and develops a value system that guides the person's action. First, an individual forms a value system within the family, and for some individuals this value system stays intact throughout life; however, for others a value system develops through life's vast experiences of facing difficult situations that require thoughtful reflection and appropriate action.

Value theory focuses on virtues that provide one with the ability to recognize and do the right thing (Beckner, 2004). The ability to do the right thing translates into virtuous action that exemplifies one's character (Beckner). In addition, value theory provides options for a leader to develop the skill in selecting principles or consequences as guidance for making ethical decisions based on a specific situation (Beckner). Over time, an individual will need experiences and wisdom to develop quality decisions without possessing basic rules or principles as guiding factors (Beckner). Deontology, teleology, and value theories form the foundation for a modern rationale of ethical thought in today's society and for today's educational leaders.

Theory of Blended Thinking

These three ethical beliefs provide an educational leader with the understanding of rules-based thinking (deontology), ends-based thinking (teleology), and care-based thinking (value theory). The limitations of these historical schools of thought require education leaders have a modern belief system to develop a personal ethics philosophy to facilitate decision-making processes in this complex society. A leader can combine a theory of personalism with servant leadership and transformational leadership to develop a cycle of moral problem-solving and moral deliberation in conjunction with other educational leaders to improve sound, reflective judgment within educational institutions. The next section explores educational leaders responding to ethical dilemmas using deontologism, consequentialism, and mixed consequentialism in an accountability era.

ETHICAL DECISION-MAKING

Educational leaders face a variety of issues that require ethical or moral decision making. Hardy (2004) cautioned educational leaders in measuring accountability by "promoting student achievement[and developing] stringent academic goals [to achieve the federal mandates of No Child Left Behind (NCLB) by stating] all students will pass state tests by 2014" (p. 17). Leaders face substantial ethical challenges to ensure students reach accountability measures by engaging learners and teachers (Starratt, 2004). The accidents of human life and human passion create situations requiring the application of moral behavior to bring about the best solution in this educational environment (Wienand, 2006). Educational leaders find themselves facing issues influenced by material selfishness at the root of human behavior (Micewski & Troy, 2007). To establish a successful learning environment, educational leaders respond to ethical dilemmas by understanding the multiple perspectives of deontologism, consequentialism, and mixed consequentialism.

Theory of Deontologism

When educational leaders face an issue that is clearly right or wrong and can use practical decision-making, the leader solves the problem using deontology (Beckner, 2004). Deontology suggests that an individual ought to respond in a certain way when faced with a black or white ethical decision (Micewski & Troy, 2007). One's moral duty is to focus on the right and wrong of a situation and help others without regard for the self (Granitz & Loewy, 2007). To solve problems, the educational leader can use the laws and rules passed by a legislative body to guide the decision-making process (Micewski & Troy). The leader responds with respect for the laws; and therefore, stays within the boundaries of ethical behavior (Micewski & Troy). The educational leader following deontoligism in ethical decision-making process considers the rights of all people. The leader considers rights and freedoms of others to form a foundation of ideas for what is ethically right (Micewski & Troy). Ultimately, justice influences all human relations when individuals interact and meet the minimal requirements for ethical behavior (Micewski & Troy).

When individual rights and freedoms collide, an educational leader can base ethical decision-making on rules and laws (Micewski & Troy, 2007). A reconciliation of individual freedom forms a "universal tenet of transcendental equality of all people" as the basis of morality for the deontologist (Micewski & Troy, p. 21). Furthermore, the deontologist's idea of universality of duty reflects the equal entitlement of others to enjoy rights and freedoms within boundaries of justice relevant for all (Micewski & Troy; Weinand, 2006) Deontologism is life affirming and does not deny the "transcendental right of every human being to strive for happiness and well-being" (Micewski & Troy, p. 23).

Theory of Consequentialism

To the educational leader, a consequentialist approach focuses the leader's perception on weighing the costs of an action compared to benefit. Consequentialism offers a leader ethical decision-making to provide "the greatest happiness for the greatest number of people" (Granitz & Loewry, 2007, p. 297). Hence, the focus on a good outcome relates "to the acting individual's (or group of individuals) notion of good and bad" (Micewski & Troy, 2007, p. 18). The educational leader's action should benefit the individual or a group of individuals, not because it is the right thing to do, but because the good of the action outweighs the right of the action (Micewski & Troy; Beckner, 2004).

Beckner (2004) said the consequence of a leader's action is the end that justifies the means. This basic relativist tenet supports the concepts of egoism and utilitarianism. Egoism is self-interest as it urges each individual to pursue personal goals to benefit the social good (Beckner). For instance, the educational leader seeks to support the individual teacher who designs classroom curriculum that keeps students engaged and improves test scores. Likewise, utilitarianism emphasizes goodness or badness of an act as determined by the end-result of the act, which can be either good or bad (Beckner). Act utilitarianism requires the action to focus upon the individual act in a particular case to determine the goodness of the act (Milde, 2002). For example, a classroom teacher focuses upon content with highly skilled students to improve student performance on grade level exams and is successful in increasing student performance. However, the same teacher focuses on content with under-skilled students and is not successful in raising these students' scores. Act utilitarianism does not include a universal perception or judgment for the goodness of the act (Beckner).

Similar to deontology, rule utilitarianism requires the action focus upon the rule as a basis for the goodness of the act (Milde, 2002). Rule utilitarianism does not guide actions to provide the best rules for people to follow all the time because the rules are good for "a single society and certain kinds of situations" (Beckner, 2004, p. 65). For instance, grade level teachers can develop curriculum guidelines that support the study of local history through visits to local farms and orchards. As the farms and orchards are sold to developers, the teachers keep their curriculum focus on local farms and orchards refusing to change direction with the community. The visits to the local farms cease and teachers resort to pictures and stories about the farms and orchards with no reference to the changes within the community.

Consequentialism focuses upon ends-based thinking compared to the rules-based thinking of deontology (Beckner, 2004). Setting an absolute goal at all cost supports justification to use any means to achieve the goal (Micewski & Troy, 2007). Hence, consequentialism focuses upon the evaluation of an action based upon the consequences of the action determined by the degree of well-being and the happiness for the greatest number of people resulting from the action (Page, 2004). In education, consequentialism can focus ethical decision-making on a current action with a future effect; ecology classes can teach that the use of fossil fuels may cause ice caps to melt leading to a rise in ocean levels and the destruction of coastal communities. Sometimes, current actions may have a detrimental effect on a great number of people (Page).

Theory of Mixed-consequentialism

Ethical decision-making includes the process of an incentive, a means, and a result (Micewski & Troy, 2007). Both deontologism and consequentialism focus on a desired result that drives an action. This dichotomy between deontology and consequentialism reflects the difference between the right action that produces the consequence versus the justification of the act to achieve the end-result (Micewski & Troy). Fortunately, an ethical theory can be deontological in the recognition of a principle of justice and consequentialist in the recognition of a principle of utility (Nandi, 2006).

An educational leader using only deontologism or consequentialism to resolve ethical dilemmas will face unresolved conflicts. The deontologist will never use whatever means it takes to arrive at the desired end-result because the deontologist reflects on the concept of moral duty (Micewski & Troy, 2007). When duties are in conflict, the educational leader hinders the desired result when using deontology as the only moral determination (Milde, 2002). Furthermore, the consequentialist must resolve conflicts by appealing to the consequences of the actions and has no alternative method of action (Milde). The deontologist, on the other hand, can rely on a long-view perspective to a short-term dilemma by keeping the individual act within a legal boundary (Micewski & Troy).

The shortcomings of deontologism and consequentialism propel leaders to re-examine the context of ethical decision-making by reflecting upon ethical dilemmas (Ladkin, 2006). To develop a sound ethical approach, ethical leaders can rely on a mixed consequentialism approach. A mixed consequentialism approach can provide a leader with the ability to focus on personal moral development and incorporate an ethical relationship into the evaluation of the dilemma (Ladkin). The educational leader can attend to the "habits of judging and jumping to conclusions" and work to remain open by inquiring into the issues behind difficult decisions (Ladkin, p. 93). The development of relationships can evoke ethical sensitivities that will respond to the context of the dilemma (Ladkin).

Recommendations

Ethical behavior is paramount in this age of accountability. Educational leaders need to be a "cohesive unit, acting for the good of the entire district despite differences" (Hardy, 2004, p. 17) existing between individuals. Individual behavior influences a code of ethical conduct that self regulates and self legislates a mantra for doing the right thing "even when it is not exclusively in our self-interest" (Micewski & Troy, 2007, p. 23) to do so. The educational leader's concern regarding relationships with humanity is the basis of an ethic of care rather than principles and perceptions of just behavior (Page, 2004).

An ethic of care focuses upon nurturing relationships with others as the guiding principle overriding all other "determinations of what is moral or right" (Page, 2004, p. 10). Educational leaders will need to take a long view of how participants in education will best resolve the issues of state and federal mandates. The best resolutions accommodate reform policies to ensure that all students learn in exemplary environments conducive to academic success (Starratt, 2004). Leaders will confront and survive the accountability. The next section relays the debate of educating special needs students in a full inclusion setting as one ethical responsibility of educational leaders. This debate reflects the need for leaders to evaluate and reason what is best culturally in an ethically diverse educational setting (Klugman & Stump, 2006).

INCLUSION: A CONTEMPORARY EDUCATIONAL ETHICS ISSUE

Educators debate the issue of full inclusion versus continuing the current model of isolated special education placements (Gallagher, 2001). Advocates for full inclusion view the issue as a moral one.

Even those who advocate for inclusion argue against full inclusion because these advocates question whether those deemed extremely medically or psychiatrically fragile should be in the regular education setting (Gallagher). In the last half of the 20th century, educators seek to identify and provide "an appropriate education for children with disabilities" (Paul, French, & Cranston-Gingras, 2001, p. 14). The education of special needs students is a "morally complex set of activities with many ethical challenges" (Paul et al., p. 14). Sensenig proposes the inclusion of special needs students in the general education programs in an ethical matter that requires a review of legal, social, and moral issues.

Legal Stance

In the early years of caring for disabled individuals, the institution-builders were promoting an ethic of care that provided decent accommodations and treatment for disabled individuals in residential facilities. However, the system fell apart and now strong accountability measures control existing residential facilities (Paul et al., 2001). In the 20th century, a new ethic of care promotes an integrated community program setting and inclusion in educational placements rather than institutions and alternative pullout programs (Paul et al.).

This advocacy came from family and friends of individuals with disabilities, and from professionals in the medical, social, and educational fields (Paul et al., 2001). These politically active individuals won Constitution arguments for the right to due process that led to successful litigation and the development of law and public policy (Paul et al.). One advocate for a morally responsible setting was Lloyd Dunn, a special education leader, whose support was for improving "the educational outcomes for children with disabilities" (Paul et al., p. 3).

The political support for children with disabilities is in the federal laws of PL 94–142. This first law, Education for All Handicapped Children Act, guarantees students with disabilities a right to receive a free, appropriate public education (FAPE) (Sack-Min, 2007). Fulfilling FAPE requirements in the least restrictive educational environment (LRE) requires leaders to education students with disabilities in the general education classroom (Rude, Paolucci-Whitcomb, & Comerford, 2005). The ideology of full inclusion promotes a responsibility of inclusive education to pursue the rights of the least restrictive environment (LRE). The values and principles of full inclusion permit all students with disabilities access to the general education classroom.

The impact of special placements and the type of services a student receives can strain local school budgets. A lack of sufficient funding can impact the implementation of the Individuals with Disabilities Education Act (IDEA) (Sack-Min, 2007). The advocacy for IDEA supports the overemphasis on the process of providing the individualized educational plan (IEP) of the student. This emphasis on process overlooks the outcomes of the services provided (Sack-Min). The democratic view of individualism, privacy, and rational choice do not support the communal view of a disability community, special needs of minorities, and inclusion (Paul et al., 2001). The moral defense of inclusion requires a vision of a society that we hope to be an educational community that supports this vision (Paul et al.).

Societal Stance

The segregation of special needs students may perpetuate the prejudices that make separate schools desirable (Gallagher, 2001). To argue against the right of all individuals to make choices in education denies the right to self-determination (Gallagher). Advocates for special needs students state scientific research should resolve the debate for or against full inclusion because a method of neutrality is beneficial to settle the issue (Gallagher). Continuing the current method of placements makes sense to the traditionalists who emphasize disabilities as real, labels as necessary, interventions required, and difficulties confronting the general education classroom (Gallagher).

Advocates for full inclusion owe that disabilities are "social constructions" of certain human attributes (Gallagher, 2001, p. 643). Perceptions become reality because disability classifications are what we make of them (Gallagher). The social construction of disabilities is what meaning society brings to bear on the perceived differences of special needs individuals (Gallagher). Likewise, the strain and stress experienced by students and teachers in classrooms every day are genuine and the differences of special needs students should be a part of the classroom environment (Gallagher). The difference of the special needs student is a social construct that has social judgment implications. The classroom context in "teaching approaches, standards, assignments and assessment format, physical arrangements and content" can accommodate the difference associated with disabilities (Gallagher, p. 645). Perceiving a disability as a difference requires educators to take a closer look at the classroom context so we can alter how we teach.

The empiricist suggests educators deliver teaching interventions in separate placements (Gallagher, 2001). These interventions include "behavior modifications, task analysis, cognitive training, medication, the commercial Direct Instruction Programs, token economies, mnemonic strategies, self-management, peer tutoring and systematic formative evaluation" (Gallagher, p. 647). However, the foundation of behavior psychology supports these interventions, and these interventions can be effective in multiple settings, not only the separate placements advocated by the empiricist (Gallagher).

The advocates for separate placement state that general education classrooms cannot accommodate all students. In addition, the advocates for separate placements express the difficulty of the regular education setting in meeting the needs of the disabled student in "large classes, inadequate resources, accountability for standards, and the reluctance of general education teachers to welcome special needs students" (Gallagher, 201, p. 649). The advocates for separate placements view the benevolent humanitarianism of a separate placement as a caring more nurturing school experience for the disabled student (Gallagher).

However, the placement of the special needs student in the general education classroom advocates for moral choice in an appropriate general education setting (Gallagher, 2001). Special needs students have the opportunity to receive an education with their peers in the general education classroom. Educators need to face the responsibility for society, schools, and classrooms that we have constructed and make the moral choice to choose with care and deliberation the moral decision to teach all children in the general education classroom (Gallagher).

Absence of Ethical Compass

Without an ethical compass, this conflict of full inclusion or specialized settings for students with disabilities would take the direction of minimal labeling or classification of students with disabilities. Students would attend general education classrooms based on age. Educators would place students unable to meet the demands of the general education setting in self-contained classrooms and disciplined appropriately.

The absence of an ethical compass would permit minimal adherence to the IDEA, FAPE, and LRE. The educator would seek to control the school community and advance individualism for the majority of the population. Educators would subdue the minority population of special needs students in self-contained classrooms to control costs with minimal specialized programs and assistance.

On occasion, special needs students would receive special programs if the courts ordered the school to provide them. The wealthy parents of special needs children will move to districts that have the best programs. The low-income parents will not know their rights and will remain silent about the student's needs (Sack-Min, 2007).

Corrective Action

An ethical educational leader coming into a hypothetical school district in which no ethical compass exists in accommodating special needs students would bring in a qualified team of special educators to classify special needs students. Educators would place the students in appropriate multiple settings: inclusion, special classes, outside placements, and residential. The special education programs would attempt to meet the needs of classified students in the appropriate setting.

For those students placed in an inclusion setting, an ethical educational leader would begin to communicate personal values regarding rights of student with disabilities and social responsibilities of the educational community. Educational leaders would begin to overcome mythologies about disabilities, unchallenged and uninformed mindsets about what education is and how it occurs, race, gender, and class-biased models of what a classroom and school should look like (Paul et al., 2001). The practical interface of special and general education students in inclusive settings would focus upon the "instrumental efficacy of instructional practices and schooling" (Paul et al., p. 15).

An educational leader will need community participation and communication to support ideas about multiple settings for students with handicapping conditions. Several public forums will bring other leaders, parents, and students on board with these new ideas. If public forums are unsuccessful, educational leaders can request a state audit to turn the school district around. Ultimately, the outcomes of practice and the promises of the law would create urgency in providing the educational support for students with disabilities (Paul et al., 2001). Ample time would overcome disputes and dilemmas regarding unfair treatment of students with disabilities. Programs for early intervention services in the regular classroom could defray costs of educating classified students (Sacks-Min, 2007).

CONCLUSION

Educating students with disabilities is a moral and social responsibility of all educators. The cost of educating these students can be very high. However, with the appropriate accommodations and the appropriate placement, students with disabilities would become an integral part of the community. The education of students with disabilities is a "morally complex set of activities with many ethical challenges" (Paul et al., 2001, p. 14). Educators have an ethical responsibility to be proactive leaders within their educational institutions (Starratt, 2004).

Ethical leadership is the responsibility of all educational leaders. Current educational leaders must seek to establish an ethical education system that ties happiness to living according to a certain social order valuing virtue relative to the whole educational society. This chapter offers a rationale for good sound judgment and practical implementation of ethical decision-making to support the social and economic influences that decisions have on the school community. Educational leaders must weigh actions against moral principles when faces with ethical dilemmas. Therefore, educational leaders need a combination of ethical decision-making to focus on personal, moral deliberation exemplifying best practice in facilitating educational decision-making.

References

Beckner, W. (2004). *Ethics for educational leaders.* San Francisco: Jossey-Bass.

Gallagher, D. J. (2001). Neutrality as a moral standpoint, conceptual confusion, and the full inclusion debate. *Disability & Society, 16*(5), 637–654.

Granitz, N., & Loewy, D. (2007). Applying ethical theories: Interpreting and responding to student plagiarism. *Journal of Business Ethics, 72,* 293–306.

Hardy, L. (2004). The ethical school board. *American School Board Journal, 191*(5), 16–19.

Klugman, C., & Stump, B. (2006). The effect of ethics training upon individual choice. *Journal of Further and Higher Education, 30*(2), 181–192.

Ladkin, D. (2006). When deontology and utilitarianism aren't enough: How Heidegger's notion of "dwelling" might help organizational leaders resolve ethical issues. *Journal of Business Ethics, 65,* 87–98.

Micewski, E. R., & Troy, C. (2007). Business ethics—Deontologically revisited. *Journal of Business Ethics, 72,* 17–25.

Milde, M. (2002). Legal ethics: Why Aristotle might be helpful. *Journal of Social Philosophy, 33*(1), 45–66.

Nandi, V. (2006). *Model of neutral inclusivity.* Retrieved from www.trinp. org/MNI/BoI/7/5/3.htm

Page, J. S. (2004). Peace education: Exploring some philosophical foundations. *International Review of Education, 50*(1), 3–15.

Patterson, W. R. (2005). The greatest good for the most fit? John Stuart Mill, Thomas Henry Huxley, and social Darwinism. *Journal of Social Philosophy, 37*(1), 72–84.

Paul, J., French, P., & Cranston-Gingras, A. (2001). Ethics and special education. *Focus on Exceptional Children, 34*(1), 1–18.

Rude, H. A., Paolucci-Whitcomb, P. E., & Comerford, S. (2005). Ethical leadership: Supporting human rights and diversity in rural communities, *Rural Special Education Quarterly, 24*(4), 26–31.

Sack-Min, J. (2007). The issues of IDEA. *American School Board Journal, 194*(3), 20–25.

Starratt, R. J. (2004). *Ethical leadership.* San Francisco: Jossey-Bass.

Vassallo, P. (2004). Notes on the methods of inquiry of Plato and Aristotle. *ETC: Review of General Semantics, 61*(3), 373–380.

Wienand, I. (2006). Descartes' Morals'. *South African Journal of Philosophy, 24*(2), 177–188).

About the Author

Dr. Neysa T. Sensenig holds an Associates in Applied Science Degree in Business Administration (AA) from the State University of New York (SUNY) Rockland Community College in Suffern; a Bachelor of Arts in English (BA) from SUNY Empire State in Saratoga Springs; a Master of Arts in English (MA) from the State University of New York at New Paltz, a Master of Arts Degree in Educational Administration (MAED) from the SUNY at Albany; and a Doctorate in Educational Leadership (Ed.D) from the University of Phoenix School of Advanced Studies.

Dr. Sensenig has been employed by New York Public Schools for the past 21 years and has been the Assistant Superintendent for Business at the Marlboro Central School District, Marlboro, New York for the last 8 years. Dr. Sensenig has also taught writing as an Adjunct Professor at SUNY Sullivan County Community College, SUNY at New Paltz, and Marist College in Poughkeepsie, NY.

Dr. Sensenig's dissertation is entitled *Impact of the 6+1 Trait Writing Model on Writing Instruction in Grades Three Through Eight.* Previously, Dr. Sensenig has published a work entitled: Theory for the Desirability of All Games in the *English Graduate Review* SUNY New Paltz, December 1993. Dr. Sensenig contributed to the Robert Penn Symposium at Western Kentucky University in April 1994 a manuscript titled: *Growth and Redemption: The Poetry of Robert Penn Warren.*

To reach Dr. Sensenig, please email: neysasensenig@msn.com.

CHAPTER 2

Have We Tipped: Are We Ready to Demand Ethical Behavior from Our Leaders?

Dr. Sheila Embry

> "The most important element of good government
> is to rule with reason and order while
> representing the ideal state"
>
> —PLATO (REPUBLIC)

The decade that began on 2000 was known by many names—the ohs, the uh ohs, the double ohs, the 2000s, the aughts, the naughts, and the zeroes (Beam, 2009; Glossary, 2010). Tragedies during the 2000s included: the 2001 earthquakes in El Salvador killing 5,565 people; the 2001 terrorist attacks within the United States (U.S.) killing 2,752 people and creating wars in Afghanistan and Iraq that have killed over 140,000 others; the 2003 Space Shuttle Columbia explosion upon reentry to the earth's atmosphere killing 7 astronauts; the 2004 Hurricane Charlie that killed 10 people and caused more than $15 billion damages; the 2004 Boxing Day tsunami in the Indian Ocean, created by an ocean earthquake measuring 9.3 on the Richter scale, killing 230,000 people in 14 countries; the 2005 Hurricanes Dennis, Katrina, Rita, and Wilma's devastations of towns and cities in the U.S. southern gulf states of Louisiana, Mississippi, Alabama, and Florida as well as in Mexico and Caribbean countries; and depending on how you counted in the decade, the 2010 earthquake in Haiti killing more than 200,000 people (America, 2009).

Despite these and other not listed here tragedies and despite thwarted terrorists' attacks (the 2001 shoe bomber over Boston, Massachusetts, the 2007 attempt to blow up John F. Kennedy airport in New York City, and the 2009 Christmas Day bombing attempt over Detroit, Michigan), scandalous stories ruled American media as 2009 closed (America, 2009). Showcasing arrogance and lack of good moral character, many people who were perceived as leaders in their fields faltered under the bright spotlight of media scrutiny. The following famous names were found in many end-of-the-decade articles:

In 2009,

- NASDAQ chair Bernie Madoff was sentenced to 150 years in prison after defrauding his clients out of more than $65 billion;

- Golfer Tiger Woods, married and father of two, was sexually linked to at least 10 other women;

- Late night talk show host David Letterman admitted to inappropriate behavior and affairs with multiple interns in his office;

- South Carolina governor Mark Sanford, married, admitted to a long-term affair with a woman from Argentina, after being discovered returning from Argentina when he told his staff he would be hiking in Appalachia.

In 2008,

- The U.S. paid $150 billion to American International Group (AIG) as a government bailout; then AIG executives distributed bonuses (including $5 million with a $15 million golden parachute to Chief Executive Officer Mark Sullivan) and attended a luxury retreat at St. Regis in Monarch Beach, California with $200,000 in rooms, $150,000 in meals, and $23,000 in spa services;

- The U.S. paid $700 billion to the banking industry as a government bailout; then executives at some banks raised their customers' interest rates and minimum payments to inappropriately high levels (e.g., raising minimum payments from $150 to $999 a month and interest rates up to 79.9%);

- New York governor and former state attorney Eliot Spitzer resigned after it was discovered that he spent thousands of dollars on prostitutes and call girls;

- Presidential hopeful senator John Edwards, married to a wife publicly struggling with breast cancer, admitted to a long-term affair that created a child. In a strange twist, Senator Edwards convinced his aide to take responsibility for the child.

- Illinois governor Rod Blageojevich was arrested on corruption charges for selling the U.S. Senate seat formerly belonging to U.S. President Barack Obama;

- Miss USA beauty pageant winner Tara Conner admitted to cocaine and alcohol abuse and was forced to check into rehabilitation center or lose her crown;

In 2007,

- NFL quarterback Michael Vick served 18 months in prison and lost his NFL salary for running an illegal dog-fighting ring;

- NASA astronaut and naval officer Lisa Nowak was arrested for attempted kidnapping with intent to terrorize Air Force Captain

Colleen Shipman, burglary of a conveyance with a weapon, battery, and attempted destruction of evidence;

- Five times Olympic gold medal winner track and field star Marion Jones forfeited all her awards and medals after admitting to performance-enhancing drug use.

In 2006,

- Enron chairman Ken Lay was indicted by a grand jury for accounting fraud and corporate abuse. He would have faced 20 to 30 years, but he died before he was sentenced;

- Lobbyist Jack Abramoff was sentenced to 5 years and 10 months for fraud;

- U. S. Representative Mark Foley resigned after admitting to sending inappropriate electronic mail and instant messages to teenage male pages;

- In 2005, television celebrity Martha Stewart served 5 months in prison for lying about the sale of her ImClone stock;

- In 2004, many prisoners were violently tortured and died at Abu Gharib prison in Iraq;

- In 2003, reporter Jayson Blair admitted to fabricating events, locations, and comments for his stories during his 4 years and 600 articles with the New York Times; and

- In 2001, U.S. Representative Gary Condit admitted to having an affair with Chandra Levy, a woman who worked for him and whose remains were found in the Washington, DC area (NBC, 2009).

A quick review of the list reminds us that leaders from all sectors—private, public, business, sports, and politics—failed the moral compass test (Thompson, 2009). The themes represented in the bullets above could each be chapters and studies of their own. For purposes of this chapter, the theme will be generally defined: an unbridled greed and an arrogance of entitlement that allowed people to ignore or deny their moral center. Yet, at the end of this decade of greed and arrogant entitlement, the author observed what is hopefully the beginning of a tipping back toward good moral character and ethical choices. There will be more about this observation at the end of this chapter.

LEADERSHIP ETHICS

Leadership

Formal leadership studies have existed for more than eighty years. Multiple models, discussions, and matrices can be categorized into these simplistic themes: (a) roles, skills, knowledge, abilities, values, and methodologies of leaders; and (b) is leadership learned or are leaders born? Basic leadership theory models include great man, trait, group, contingency, transactional, and transformational (Rost, 1993).

Great man theory, developed around the 19th century, held that leaders were born not made. Leaders were born into class positions that dictated leadership behavior. *Trait theory* was based on leadership in the 1920s through 1940s that posited that leadership was personality and skills based. *Group theory* emerged in the 1950s with the theory that if managers gave attention to their employees, employees would increase their production and performance. Famous group theories included Maslow's hierarchy of needs and McGregor's Theory X and Theory Y (Rost, 1993).

Contingency theory was based on leadership from the 1960s forward and included exchange, behavioral, path-goal, normative, situational, and principle-centered theories. It was not based on traits but rather on characteristics; the idea being that the leaders' characteristics must have relevance to the followers, activities, and goals of the groups. *Transactional theory* was based on leadership from the late 1970s and was the first one listed as 21st century leadership. It was based on a political exchange, barter system. Because of the give to get dynamic, most transactional relationships are short-lived. *Transformational theory* was based on leaders and collaborators working together on mutual purposes to effect real change (Rost, 1993).

Leaders of organizations and governmental agencies have started abandoning the transactional (i.e., give and take) approaches to leadership and are adopting transformational approaches (Berkley, 2008). Transformational strategies were reciprocal, relied on trust, empowered employees, and encouraged ownership of organizational goals (Colbert, Kristoff-Brown, & Bradley, 2008). Burns and Bass, known for their work in transformational and visionary leadership, focused on strategies for supervisors to enhance the motivation, morale, and performance of employees. Collaborative, transformational leadership theory emerged as a way to influence employees' perceptions, values, expectations, and aspirations. Because of the trust, empowerment, and engagement components, transformational leaders should have a high level of leadership ethics to ensure the highest level of ethical employee performance (Berkley, 2008).

In an analysis of poor leadership, Williams (2005) suggested, "If the leader is disengaged or absent, followers find themselves in a state of disorder and confusion with little hope of a vision for a way out of the mayhem" (pp. 6–7). Vivar (2006) warned managers not to leave employees feeling lost or abandoned. Several researchers showed workers strongly preferred visible communicators who were present and available (Rosengren, Athlin, & Segesten, 2007; Rouse, 2009).

A review of supervisor leadership literature indicated federal government employees regularly study supervisor and employee performance. Biannual studies and research were conducted to investigate the effectiveness of specific projects, but an analysis revealed a significant theoretical gap in the existing governmental literature. Historically, agency research lacked a conceptual framework to ground the analysis within the leadership literature. Data analysis consisted of basic frequency information with an executive summary. Few studies included an analysis of results within the context of contemporary theory, thereby hampering governmental leaders in the identification of meaningful, valid, and executable recommendations for improvement.

Ethics

Inside each of the theories listed above are the key tenets, components, and major proponents. In value-based and principle-centered leadership theories, the key tenets include integrity, trustworthiness, listening, respect, courage, persistence, and modeling ethical leadership examples (Rost, 1993). It is in these tenets that leadership ethics resides. According to Woodruff, "ethics and values are essential ingredients in the makeup of today's global leaders. These leadership values should include behavioral integrity, which is leading by example, where the words of the leader match their personal actions. Leaders with a solid ethical foundation live this example which adds to the credibility of the leader and the organization" (2009, p. 11).

Leaders have a responsibility to their employees, to their organizations, and to society (Rouse & Schuttler, 2009). Leaders must be trusted and respected or it will not matter what they say. Talented employees will not continue to work for supervisors who are unethical and cannot be trusted. Trust has to be earned. One of the ways to build trust is to practice open communication, visibility, and attentiveness (Schuttler, 2010).

Information is key and should be shared whenever possible. "Positive visibility must be displayed in all actions—including e-mails, memorandums, meetings, and casual conversations—regardless of the audience" (Schuttler, 2010, p. 37). Attentiveness is being proactive, listening to your employees and being aware and in tune with what is going on around you. The attentiveness and visibility of leaders influence employees' perception of a supervisor's communication skills.

Kerfoot (2007) indicated leader engagement, as well as disengagement, was contagious. If leaders were not careful, they could inadvertently communicate poor attitudes and behaviors to their employees. Treat your employees professionally with dignity and respect, and strengthen your communications with your employees and you will improve your working relationships, your employees' morale, and your organizations' performances (Schuttler, 2010).

STUDY

Below are partial findings from a 2009 dissertation presented in partial fulfillment of requirements for a doctor of management degree. The online survey was conducted from May 31, 2009, through July 6, 2009, at a large federal agency within a United States cabinet-level department. The purpose of the current mixed-methods study was to examine the relationship between leadership, communication, and employee performance within one federal agency directorate. The mixed-methods study included a quantitative test of the relationship between leadership communication and employee performance and a qualitative exploration of recommendations to enhance communication and leadership competencies.

The descriptive design provided clarification within the study with detailed characteristics identified in the study (Cone & Foster, 2006). The goal was to test the correlation between the predictor variables of perceived supervisor leadership and communication and the criterion variable of employee performance. The population included national employees, supervisors, and executives who work within one federal agency directorate headquartered in Washington, DC.

Data Collection

Participating leaders were located within one directorate comprised of 201 field offices throughout the United States. Demographic data collection included: (a) the division and location where the survey respondent worked, (b) the rank of either general service or senior executive service the survey respondent held, and (c) whether the survey respondent supervised people. Open coding simplified the examination of the written data to identify correlations between responses. The mixed methodology study was conducted to assess the correlations between supervisor leadership, supervisor communication, and employee performance.

Instrumentation

The Supervisor Leadership Communication Inventory (SLCI) developed by Rouse and Schuttler (2009) was used for the study with the authors' permission. The instrument was used to measure the study variables in a two-dimensional grid showing how supervisor leadership and communication could predict employee behavior. The SLCI contained 53 questions to measure supervisor leadership and employee performance, 3 demographic questions, and 3 open-ended questions to allow the participants to offer comments, suggestions, and recommendations for better leadership communication and better employee performance. The SLCI was tested for reliability several times (Rouse, 2009) with consistently high reliabilities reported (Rouse & Kaplan, 2008; Rouse & Schuttler, 2009; Schuttler & Rouse, 2008).

Agency officials granted approval to distribute survey announcement fliers in employee break rooms and cafeterias and through private social networks such as *Linked In, Facebook,* and *My Space.* One Uniform Resource Locator (URL) provided an incentive question asking for the name of the participants' favorite charity and stating that the author would provide one dollar for each completed survey. The participants chose the American Cancer Society as their most listed charity. Participants who chose the other URL to complete the survey were asked to list their names and mailing addresses if they wished to participate in the Starbucks $20.00 gift cards raffle. Personal information was listed voluntarily and was not a requirement to complete the survey. The winning survey respondents, each 25th person, received gift cards. All gift cards were mailed to the winners by July 20, 2009.

The data were collected over 35 days through secure, exclusive URLs. The URL sites hosting the survey recorded each participant's IP address and allowed only one response from each IP address. Each survey result was recorded on one spreadsheet with the participant code as the row heading and the question number as the column heading. Participant codes were used to maintain confidentiality. The spreadsheet was the main data depository of all survey data collected.

Findings

Response Rate. Based on the Sample Size Calculator with a confidence level of 95% for a population of 7,683 employees, the study required 366 completed surveys to obtain its targeted population (Creative

Research System, 2009). After 35 days of data collection, 435 individuals participated in the study. Eighty-seven percent (87%) (n = 378) completed the survey while 13% (n = 57) provided partial responses. With 378 completed surveys, the study exceeded the target population by 12 respondents. Fifty-seven (57) participants began the survey but ended before completing it. Each of the 57 participants stopped their survey at demographic questions at the beginning. The first question was asking the participants to identify the division where they worked. Each of the participants who opted out of the survey left before completing the first demographic question.

Distribution Methods. The URL site listing the charity question had 227 participants (52.2%) while the URL site listing the gift card raffle had 208 participants (47.8%). Except for the questions regarding the charity and the Starbucks gift cards raffle, all information on each URL was identical. As illustrated in Figure 1, findings show significant differences (t (380) = 3.66, p = .001) between the average supervisor leadership score for individuals who responded to the survey after receiving the charity invitation (M = 3.04, SD = .72) as opposed to the responding to the flier (M = 2.90, SD = .80).

Significant differences (t (380) = 4.00, p = .001) were found between the average supervisor communication score for individuals who responded to the survey after receiving the charity invitation (M = 2.99, SD = .78) as opposed to those responding to the flier (M = 2.82, SD = .88). There were significant differences (t (380) = 3.56, p = .001) between the average outcome score for individuals who responded to the survey after receiving the charity invitation (M = 3.16, SD = .80) as opposed to those responding to the flier (M = 3.00, SD = .97). There were no significant differences (t (380) = -.55, p = .58) between the average employee performance score for individuals who responded to the survey after receiving the charity invitation (M = 3.13, SD = .56) as opposed to those responding to the flier (M = 3.15, SD = .62).

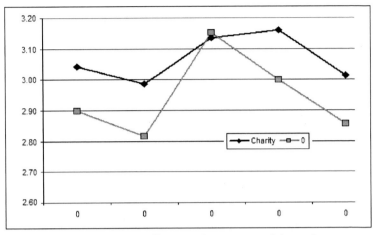

Figure 1. T tests showing differences between participants' responses within two URLs.

Model Variables

The variables were computed using a codebook. Negatively phrased items were reflected, and items were subsequently summed to produce composite scores for supervisor leadership, supervisor communication, and employee performance. The skewness of all three constructs was near zero, indicating the variables were suitable for inferential statistical analysis.

A reliability analysis was conducted to verify the reliability of the SLCI items. The supervisor leadership and communication constructs had high reliability while the employee performance and organizational outcome measures had acceptable reliability. The SLCI's overall Cronbach's alpha was .82. The findings indicated the measures were sufficiently reliable for conducting the statistical analysis. Three professionals subjected the data from the three open-ended questions to content analysis by coding. One coder had a Doctorate in Management degree, one coder had a Doctorate in Education degree, and the final coder had a Master's of Arts degree.

Using the a priori approach, themes were provided by the Federal Human Capital Survey and Best Places to Work in Federal Government Studies (Partnership for Public Service, 2007).

Correlational Analysis

Senior leadership. The purpose of Research Question 1 (RQ1) was to investigate the correlation between senior leaders' leadership and employees' performance. The scores for each participant were plotted on a two-dimensional grid. As shown in Figure 2 on the following page, the scatter plot reveals a strong positive relationship between the two variables. Supervisor leadership was significantly correlated ($r_{(1,379)}$ = .63, p < .01) with employee performance. High

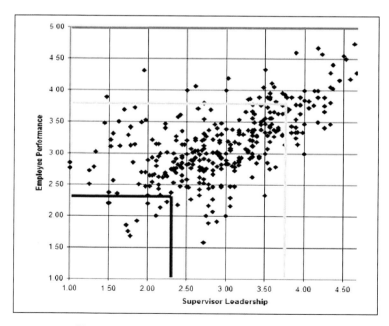

Figure 2. Scatter plot of supervisor leadership and employee performance.

levels of supervisor leadership were associated with high employee performance, and low supervisor leadership was significantly associated with low employee performance. The data provided strong support for the alternative hypothesis that a significant correlation exists between supervisor leadership and employee performance.

A view of the above scatter plot in color would reveal that the lower left corner is the red zone grid, the middle section is the yellow zone grid, and the upper right section is the green zone grid. With a traffic light metaphor, the model's framework allows managers to identify critical concerns (red), as well as elements needing to be watched (yellow), and other elements working well (green) (Schuttler, 2010). The majority of the study's respondents rated the agency in a mid-range (yellow) performance zone, indicating opportunities for improvement.

Employees admitted to sometimes feeling lost and confused, and to providing less than excellent performances because of their floundering. Many employees attributed these feelings to their perceptions that leaders were making seat-of-the-pants, by-the-gut decisions or trendy fad decisions without consideration of the agency's strategic goals and plans. Employees also wrote about inconsistent leadership depending on where they worked and about ineffective explanations for ever-changing directions and assignments (Schuttler, 2010).

Employee Performance. An open-ended question pertained to how, if at all, leaders could improve employee performance. Responses to the question were categorized using themes listed in *Laws of Communication: The Intersection Where Leaders Meet Employee Performance* (Schuttler, 2010). Theme categories included: (a) trust, (b) visibility, (c) education, (d) change, (e) mentoring/coaching, (f) attentiveness, (g) morale, and (h) other.

Being more visible accounted for 21% of the participants' responses to the second open-ended question, followed closely by attentiveness (19%) and education (17%). Other response percentages for the question included trust (10%), mentoring/coaching (6%), morale (5%), and change (2%). The category of other (20%) was divided into subcategories. The participants' responses to the category of other included: (a) hiring the correct people, (b) delivering consistent messages to all employees, (c) training, (d) everything is okay, and (e) cannot fix it. Providing consistent messages to all employees was the participants' response 45% of the time in the category of other, followed by everything is okay (20%), and hire correct people (16%), decrease email (11%), and cannot fix it (8%).

Gap Analysis

Approximately 80% of the participants who responded were field employees, and approximately 20% of the participants who responded were employees working at headquarters. Field employees who participated in the study had consistently lower perceptions than employees who participated in the study from headquarters. As shown in Figure 3 on the following page, the statistical comparison of the means of headquarters and field participants indicates highly significant differences.

Study Summary

A purpose of the mixed-methods study was to discover relationships between supervisor leadership and employee performance. Research Question 1 asked, what relationship, if any, exists between senior leaders' leadership and employees' performance. The $H1_O$ stated there is no significant correlation between supervisor leadership and employee performance. The $H1_A$ stated there is a significant correlation between supervisor leadership and employees' performance. Quantitative responses indicated that supervisors' leadership was sig-

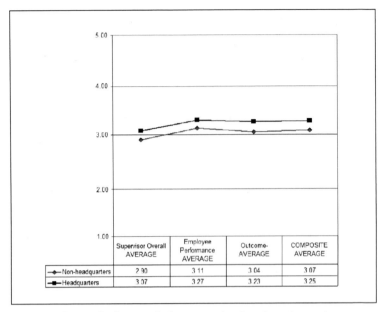

Figure 3. Gap analysis comparing headquarter and non-headquarter participants' perceptions.

nificantly correlated ($r = .63$, $p = .001$) with employee performance. High levels of supervisor leadership were associated with high employee performance, and low supervisor leadership was significantly associated with low employee performance.

The results aligned with conclusions in previous studies that supervisors' leadership affects their employees' performance (Bernerth, 2007; Bohn & Grafton, 2002; Kerfoot, 2007; Major, Davis, & Germano, 2007). Supervisor leadership includes employee motivation, commitment, encouragement, integrity, fair management, creativity, professional development, and employee empowerment (Partnership for Public Service, 2007). Grindley (2009) noted the Federal Government's supervisors and leaders had the responsibility to reestablish a sense of pride into government employees, to create incentives for motivation and commitment, and to encourage employees.

Colbert et al. (2008) stated supervisor leadership was the basic act of engaging others to follow by including reciprocal strategies, trust, and employee engagement. Lunney (2009) stated employees who were fully engaged had higher opinions of their supervisors' abilities while employees with lower engagement had less favorable opinions of their supervisors' abilities. Bohn and Grafton (2002) and Brodsky and Newell (2009) showed a strong correlation between supervisor leadership and employee performance. Correlations of leadership and employee performance were found in studies from the Ballenstedt (2009), Isley (P. Isley, personal communication, March 17, 2008), Rosenberg (2009a, 2009b), Partnership for Public Service (2007), USMSPB (2008), and the current study.

An open-ended question asked, how, if at all, could leaders improve employee performance? Though responses were qualitative, they neatly fit into an a priori system of themes by the Best Places to Work in Federal Government (Partnership for Public Service, 2007). Themes and responses included: (a) effective leadership (56%), (b) performance-based rewards and advancement (15%), (c) teamwork (10%), (d) strategic management (6%), (e) employee skills/mission match (1%), and (f) other (12%). The category of other was divided into subcategories that included (a) provide more training (71%), (b) nothing can/should be done (12%), (c) leave the agency (12%), and (d) remove the union (5%).

According to the U.S. Office of Personnel Management's Handbook (2001), employee performance is defined as distinct from productivity and includes employee morale and job satisfaction (O'Connor, 2006). Kerfoot (2007) determined that, if supervisors and leaders were engaged, their employees were more likely to be engaged. O'Connor (2006) stated low employee morale was not a problem with motivation but with a lack of job certainty and mission support failure. To improve employee morale and employee performance, supervisors should communicate more about the employees' position within the organization's overall mission and assist with training opportunities and other strategies to address skill deficiencies. Major, et al determined relationships between supervisors and employees were one of the critical elements for positive employee morale and performance (2007). Colbert, et al (2008) found that when supervisors exhibited a positive influence by motivation, inspiration, and commitment to concern for employees' intellectual opportunities and professional needs, employees' morale increased and employees were more engaged in the organizations' vision, mission, strategies, and goals.

Quantitative responses in the current study indicated field employees had consistently lower perceptions of supervisors than employees located in headquarters. The statistical comparison of the means of both headquarters and field showed highly significant differences. The participants included approximately 80% from the field and 20% from headquarters, a similar distribution as in the current employee population of 87% field employees, and 13% headquarters employees ("agency," personal communication, July 18, 2009). The qualitative responses were similar to responses that midlevel managers' perceptions of supervisors' communication differed significantly from the perceptions of frontline employees (Rouse, 2009). As senior leaders create communication strategies, they should remember that what they consider sufficient in headquarters was not considered sufficient in field offices.

In addition, there was a gap indicating lower perceptions between those who responded from electronic invitations and those who responded from paper invitations. Those who responded from paper invitations rated significant differences between the average supervisor leadership score and the average supervisor communication score. However, there were no significant differences rated on the average employee performance score.

Study Conclusion

The purpose of the current study was to confirm findings in previous studies of relationships between leadership, supervisor communication, employee performance, and organizational performance (Ballenstedt, 2009; Partnership for Public Service, 2007; USMSPB, 2008). Recommendation #1 was to replicate the study agency-wide for an accurate assessment in communication and leadership, targeted relationship building, and training for all leaders. The second recommendation included a suggestion for further research within other government agencies and private organizations. The recommendations for further research will add to the body of leadership, communication, employee performance, and organizational outcomes knowledge.

If senior leaders and supervisors increase their leadership and communication knowledge and skills, they can increase employee and organizational performance. By developing both sides of the two-dimensional grid, leaders are more likely to be able to move their agencies and organizations from the yellow zone to the green zone. Within the green zone, employees feel valued and become self-directed. Within the green zone, employees "are responsible for performance improvement, [can] modify goals as conditions change, [and] are champions of change" (Schuttler, 2010, p. 14). Employees who feel valued and have higher morale are more likely to feel more engaged in their organizations and are more likely to give higher rating to their performance and their organization's performance (Brodsky & Newell, 2009; USMSPB, 2008).

CONCLUSION

Ethical leaders model integrity, trustworthiness, listening, respect, courage, and persistence regularly (Rost, 1993). Three methods to model ethical leadership include open communication, visibility, and attentiveness. Leaders who continue to model these characteristics will add credibility to their teams and the organizations (Schuttler, 2010).

To model ethical communication, a leader must be open and honest. A leader should simply state if information cannot be shard instead of making up a lie "Hiding information makes people suspicious and compromises your integrity" (Kaplan, 2010, ¶7).

To model ethical visibility, leaders should make walking around and having discussions with people part of their regular routine. If they only walk around when things are going wrong, they will be perceived as looking for trouble. As well, sitting in the office and sending emails may be easier and more efficient. However, leaders will have much more credibility with others if they get up, walk around, and look people in the eye, especially when delivering bad news. "Leaders should remember that the manner and tone in which an organization communicates is one of the main drivers for how the business will perform" (Kaplan, 2010, ¶9).

To model ethical attentiveness, leaders should actively listen to team members, assist them with their career development, and set an ethical example for them to follow. Leaders should not ask team members to work long hours unless they are seen working long hours. Leaders should not ask team members to take pay cuts or cuts in hours if they are not willing to take the same cuts. Leaders should walk the walk they want their teams to walk, and walk the talk they are sharing with the team (Kaplan, 2010).

Is the common sense guidance listed above significant, substantial, and relevant in view of the greed and arrogant entitlement characteristic that was so prevalent in the last decade? Should leaders make conscious decisions to make ethical choices even when they are more difficult? Should leaders make conscious decisions to make ethical choices when others around them are making unethical decisions for short-term gains? To answer this question, please consider an event observed toward the end of 2009 that may perhaps be a tip back toward rewarding ethical behavior.

Tipping is a term made famous in the 2000 book, *The Tipping Point: How Little Things Can Make a Big Difference* (Gladwell, 2002). Gladwell posited that there are patterns and factors that define each influential trend. His theory was that new ideas are constantly being introduced, and that there are three simple rules that illustrate what may 'tip' an idea or product into popularity. They are: (a) the Law of the Few, (b) the Stickiness Factor, and (c) the Power of Context. The Law of the Few stated that for an idea or product to reach the tipping point, a few key types of people must champion it. The stickiness factor is harder to define. Stickiness is unconventional, unexpected, and can be contrary to common wisdom. The power of context is very important when determining what tips an idea or product into popularity. Gladwell defined context broadly including even minute variations in social groups, the environment, community, or neighborhood (Gladwell, 2002).

These factors were in place at the season finale of Survivor: Samoa. The CBS television show was the first reality television show. It was developed in 2000, and it has created a new genre for television. Survivor has been on the air for 10 years and is shown in more than 45 countries. There have been 301 contestants and 19 winners. The premise of the show is to place between 16 to 20 people, per season, in competitive tribe-settings in different exotic locales (e.g. Fiji, Samoa, Thailand, Australian Outback, Africa, Marquesas, Pearl Island, Guatemala, Palau, Panama, Cook Islands, China, Gabon, Micronesia, Tocantins, and the Amazon) (Denhart, 2009).

Survivor's logo is *Outwit, Outplay, and Outlast.* In the early seasons, contestants generally depended on outplaying the other contestants. In recent seasons, there was a shift towards outwitting. However, outwitting has become defined as lies, manipulation, theft, and sabotage. No Survivor contestant has been perceived as having less ethics than Russell Hanz, runner-up in the Survivor: Samoa season (Denhart, 2009).

From the first day, Russell lied to all of his contestants telling them that he was a fireman in New Orleans who lost all his family in Hurricane Katrina. He was a millionaire oilman from Daytona, Texas. He manipulated contestants by lying continually and by making promises that he did not keep. He sabotaged his own tribe by emptying all their water canteens, and opening cages holding chickens so that he could take advantage of the chaos. He was openly contemptuous of his team members calling them weak and ignorant (Denhart, 2010).

Watching Russell Hanz on Survivor: Samoa was a great object lesson of a person playing the short game with no regard for personal or professional ethics or his personal legacy. He made it clear that he wanted to be the puppet master, the master manipulator who controlled people for his own devious plan. He bragged about it often.

Russell forgot about the long game. Many of the people he had lied to, tricked, and manipulated were placed on the jury that would vote between Russell and Natalie White to determine who would win the $1 million and the title of 'Sole Survivor.' Natalie was a Survivor contestant with a plan to arrive at the end of the game without abandoning her ethics and integrity.

A nail-biting season finale on December 21, 2009, provided a surprising ending that should be the first tipping point towards determining that ethics is an essential characteristic for leaders in the 2010 decade. Watching the jury vote for Natalie as the 19th Sole Survivor was also a vote against greed and entitled arrogance. Russell Hanz' response to losing the title and the money was one of disbelief. He could not understand how the jury he had tricked, lied to, manipulated, and voted off, could vote against him. Russell's arrogance was so strong that he offered to pay Natalie $100,000 for the title of 'Sole Survivor.' When she declined to give up her title, Russell created a website, www.Russellgotscrewed.com (Denhart, 2010).

By his actions to date, it appears that Russell has not learned the lesson of the jury vote. Yet, it is this author's hope that others did notice. It was a small, much needed spark in an otherwise disappointing decade.

References

A scandalous decade: Sex, stealing, and scheming. (2009. December 24). *NBC Philadelphia.* Retrieved from www.nbcphiladelphia.com/entertainment/celebrity/NATL-A-Scandalous-Decade—70188212.html

America's best history: US T=timeline—2000s. (2009). Retrieved from http://americasbesthistory. com/abhtimeline2000.html

Ballenstedt, B. (2009, March 9). Obama urged to reconsider pledge to thin management ranks. *Government Executive.* Retrieved from www.governmentexecutive.com/story_page_pf.cfm?articleid+42219

Beam, C. (2009, December 19). The Uh-Ohs: What should we call the last decade? *Slate.* Retrieved from www.slate.com/id/2239014.

Berkley, J. (2008). *Leadership handbook of management and administration.* Grand Rapids, MI: Baker Books.

Bernerth, J. (2007). Is personality associated with perceptions of LMX? An empirical study. *Leadership & Organization Development Journal, 28*(7), 613. Retrieved from *ProQuest* database.

Bohn, J. G., & Grafton, D. (2002). The relationship of perceived leadership behaviors to organizational efficacy [Electronic version]. *Journal of Leadership & Organizational Studies, 9*(2), 65.

Brodsky, R., & Newell, E. (2009). Memo to the president-elect. *Government Executive, 41*(1), 25–30.

Colbert, A., Kristoff-Brown, A., & Bradley, B. (2008). CEO transformational leadership: The role of goal importance congruence in top management teams. *Academy of Management Journal, 51*(1), 81–96. Retrieved from *EBSCOhost* database.

Cone, J. D., & Foster, S. L. (2006). *Dissertations and theses from start to finish: Psychology and related fields.* New York: Springer Publications.

Creative Research System. (2009). *Sample size calculator.* Retrieved from www.surveysystem.com/sscalc.htm

Denhart, A. (2009). 'Natalie" claims Survivor Crown: New reality show millionaire refuses to sell 'sole survivor ' title. Retrieved from www.msnbc.msn.com/id/34468042/ns/entertainment-reality_tv/

Gladwell, M. (2002). *The tipping point: How little things can make a big difference.* New York: Little Brown Publishing, Inc.

Grindley, L. (2009, February 9). Federal workforce needs some tender loving care, says Clinton official. *National Journal.* Retrieved from www.govexec.com/story_page_pf.cfm?articleid=41997

Kaplan, J., Rouse, R., & Schuttler, R. (2010) *Leadership coaching tip: Gut wrenching decisions: How ethically do you behave in a crisis?* Retrieved from www.integralleadershipreview.com/archives/2010-01/2010-01-coaching-tip.php

Kerfoot, K. (2007). Staff engagement: It starts with the leader [Electronic version]. *Nursing Economics, 25*(1), 47–48.

Lunney, K. (2009). The briefing. *Government Executive, 41*(2), 7.

O'Connor, T. (2006, September 29). Employee morale (esprit de corps) programs. *Megalinks in Criminal Justice.* Retrieved from www.apsu.edu/oconnort/4000/4000lect04.htm

Partnership for Public Service. (2007). *Best places to work in the federal government 2007.* Retrieved from http://bestplacestowork.org/BPTW/rankings

Plato. (360BCE). *The republic.* Retrieved from http://classics.mit.edu/Plato/republic.html

Rosenberg, A. (2009a, January 26). TSA employees give management low marks. *Government Executive.* Retrieved from www.govexec.com/story_page_pf.cfm?articleid=41875

Rosenberg, A. (2009b, March 5). Advocates say DHS managers, rank-and-file are dissatisfied with personnel policies. *Government Executive.* Retrieved from www.govexec.com/story_page_ pf.cfm?articleid=42201

Rosengren, K., Athlin, E., & Segesten, K. (2007). Presence and availability: Staff conceptions of nursing leadership on an intensive care unit [Electronic Version]. *Journal of Nursing Management, 15,* 522–529.

Rost, J. (1993). *Leadership for the Twenty-first Century.* New York: Praeger Publishers.

Rouse, R. A. (2009). Ineffective participation: Reactions to absentee and incompetent nurse leadership in an intensive care unit. *Journal of Nursing Management, 17*(4), 463–473. doi: 10.1111/j.1365–2834. 2009. 00981.x

Rouse, R. A., & Kaplan, J. B. (2008). *Avoiding haphazard assessment: An empirical test of a diagnostic instrument measuring healthcare leader communication.* Manuscript submitted for publication.

Rouse, R., & Schuttler, R. (2009). *Crisis communication: A mixed method study of supervisor leadership and employee performance during the 2008–2009 financial crisis.* Retrieved from www.SLCI.com

Schuttler, R. (Ed.). (2010). *Laws of communication: The intersection where leadership meets employee performance.* Hoboken, NJ: John Wiley & Sons.

Schuttler, R., & Rouse, R. (2008). *Intensive care unit supervisor communication inventory survey results.* (Available Organizational Troubleshooter, LLC, 15319 Rompel Trail, San Antonio, TX 78232)

Thompson, L. (2009). *The moral compass: Leadership for a free world.* New York: Information Age Publishing, Inc.

U.S. Merit Systems Protection Board. (2008). *The power of federal employee engagement.* Retrieved from www.mspb.gov/netsearch/viewdocs.aspx?docnumber=379024&version=379721

U.S. Office of Personnel Management. (2001, September). Workforce compensation and performance service. *A handbook for measuring employee performance: Aligning employee performance with organizational goals.* U.S. Office of Personnel Management. Performance Management and Incentive Awards Division (PMD–013). Washington, DC: U.S. Government Printing Office.

Vivar, C. (2006). Putting conflict management into practice: A nursing case study [Electronic version]. *Journal of Nursing Management, 14,* 201–206.

What should we call this decade anyways? (2010) *Glossary of Mathematical Mistakes.* Retrieved http://members.cox.net/mathmistakes/decade.htm.

Williams, D. F. (2005). *Toxic leadership in the U.S. Army.* Retrieved from www.strategicstudiesinstitute.army.mil/pdffiles/ksil3.pdf

Woodruff, T. (2009). Normative leadership types and organizational performance: A case for authoritative performance. In C. A. Lentz (Ed.). *The refractive thinker: Vol. 1 An anthology of doctoral writers (1st ed., pp. 1–14).* Las Vegas, NV; Lentz Leadership Institute, LLC.

About the Author

 Washington DC author Dr. Sheila Embry holds three nationally accredited degrees; a Baccalaureate in Business Administration (BA) from McKendree College; a Master of Arts (MA) in Human Resources Development from Webster University, and a Doctorate of Management in Organizational Leadership (DM) from the University of Phoenix School of Advanced Studies. She also holds a certificate from Spencerian College (where she was named Outstanding Alum) and four certificates from the Federal Law Enforcement Training Center.

'Dr. She' is a directorate Training Unit Chief within USCIS. Previous assignments included Branch Chief for Service Center Operations, Program Manager for USCIS Academy, Supervisor, and Immigration Officer for Fraud Detection and National Security, and Supervisor and Adjudications Officer for California Service Center. Previous temporary assignments included Field Office Director with the American Embassy in Kingston, Jamaica; and citizenship details in El Paso, Texas, and Los Angeles, California.

Before working for USCIS, Dr. She worked as a Local Projects Coordinator for Congressman Romano L. Mazzoli; with the Hilton Hotels Corporation in Louisville, Kentucky and Irvine, California; and The Irvine Company in Irvine, California.

To reach Dr. Sheila Embry for information on any of these topics, please e-mail: drembry@ymail.com.

CHAPTER 3

Physician Cultural Attitudes towards Hospice Services

Dr. Karleen Yapp

Beneficence is a fundamental concept of medicine, which embodies the notion *above all, do no harm* (Walker, 2007). Beauchamp and Childress (1994) defined beneficence as the "moral obligation to act for the benefit of patients in balancing benefit, risk, and cost of all treatment" (as cited in Stroud, 2002, p. 180). While this principle illustrates the healthcare professional's duty to contribute to the patient's welfare, the principle becomes convoluted when the wishes of the patient directly conflict with that of the physician (Beauchamp & Childress). Beauchamp and Childress further argued both beneficence and autonomy carry equal weight in the bioethical decision making process; the physician's goal of treatment or treatment options must be understood and the autonomous decisions of a competent patient must be respected. The concept of hospice has challenged the ethical principle of beneficence and brought into question the issue of patient autonomy based on its founding principle of foregoing aggressive, possibly life sustaining treatment, for a good death (Lobar, Youngblut, & Brooten, 2006; Morrison, Maroney-Galin, Kralovec, & Meier, 2005; O'Gorman, 1998; Ruhnke et al., 2000).

Physicians regularly encounter cultural dilemmas associated with prognostication and discussion with regard to end of life treatment options, especially hospice care. The physician's role as the head of the multidisciplinary healthcare team requires the physician to develop a sense of personal and professional identity to lead effectively within individually established cultural boundaries. Patients rely on a physician's professional opinion to determine the course of medical care; however, end of life issues represent the largest barrier to communication between patients and physicians. Additionally, the patient's family often plays a pivotal role in end of life decision-making, relying on their understanding of their loved ones diagnosis, prognosis, and alternate treatment options provided by the primary care physician (Cherlin et al., 2005). Recent studies on caregiver-physician communication conducted among patients and families revealed infrequent discussions of hospice by physicians, inability to share prognosis, physician's lack of understanding of patient's preference, and the exclusion of patient and family in the decision-making process (Caserett & Quill, 2007; Cherlin et al.; Gauthier, 2005; Hickman, 2002; Larkin & Schotsmans, 2007; Matzo, 2004; Ruhnke et al., 2000). Consequently, the physicians and their patients may not have a collective understanding of the meaning of illness or death, nor do they have a united approach to end of life issues when they arise.

Culture is defined as "the behavior patterns, arts, beliefs, institutions, and all other products of human work and thought, especially as expressed in a particular community" (American Heritage Dictionary, 1994). Devore and Schlesinger (1995) argued culture "often refers to the fact that human groups differ in how they structure their behavior, their worldview, their perspectives on the rhythms of life and their concept of the essential nature of the human condition" (p. 903). Contributing to the complexity of culture are the social, economic, and political forces inherent within any society that alter the way in which culture is viewed. An individual's cultural beliefs and values are main determinants of decision-making and ultimately create behavioral patterns in society. The influence of culture in decision-making is evident in all aspects of an individual's life; however, culture may become more pronounced during end of life decision-making. Without the proper context in which to base end of life discussions, the intersect of diverse cultures and healthcare policy may result in misunderstanding with regard to treatment decisions, lack of trust in the healthcare team, and tense interactions. Recent studies demonstrated deeply embedded cultural beliefs are prevalent throughout the healthcare system, influencing physician practice and the application of technology for terminally ill patients. (Hern, Koenig, Moore, & Marshall, 1998; Lapine, Wang-Cheng, Goldstein, Nooney, Lamb, & Derse, 2001). Additional studies revealed that cultural variations between healthcare providers and their patients may affect the attitudes towards death, how patients and their families approach end of life decision-making, and the treatment received immediately preceding death (Kawaga-Singer & Blackhall, 2001).

This study sought to ascertain if cultural beliefs influence the decision-making process of a physician in referring a patient to hospice services. This qualitative, phenomenological study used the modified Van Kaam method by Moustakas (1994) and semi-structured interviews to explore the influence of cultural beliefs on physician referrals to hospice services. A purposive sample of 14 physicians practicing in the Mercer County, NJ area for approximately two or more years using the American Medical Association database of practicing physicians was used.

Findings

Based upon the analysis of data provided by the 14 participants in the study, the following five themes emerged from the data gathered during the interview process: (a) physician personal perspectives,

(b) physician perspectives on culture, (c) physician perspectives on hospice care, (d) communication with patients, and (e) physician training and experience.

Physician Personal Perspectives

The physicians in this study expressed many personal views with regard to death and dying, acculturation and the role of a physician, and the skills required to communicate effectively in end of life circumstances with a patient and their family. Nearly 72% of the participants interviewed directly mentioned death as a natural and inevitable part of the process of life. In dealing with communication and decisions regarding the end of life circumstances of a patient, some participants felt that the role of the physician is to remain analytical and scientific, and focused on their job as a physician, to present the best options and effectively communicate the situation to the patient, regardless of their own cultural beliefs (28.6%). Nearly 36% of the physicians interviewed perceived that a personal acculturation experience enabled this ability to disconnect their own beliefs when making decisions for their patients, helping them to better perceive the patients needs through the culture and background of the patient rather than their own culture. The physician's personal skill in terms of bedside manner, humility, and communication, are determining factors affecting the physician's ability to effectively and positively communicate with the patients and achieve a positive result (21.4%). The perspectives presented in theme 1 seemed to allow for increased ease of communication and decreased conflict between patient and physician. These perspectives enable the participants to focus on their job and the needs of the patient, by having a greater understanding and respect for the dignity of life and the individual, regardless of cultural differences.

Casarett and Quill (2007) identified lack of communication skills and the inability to predict the life expectancy as the two major factors that impede hospice referrals and complicate the patient-physician relations. The participants identified patient-physician communication as a significant barrier during end of life discussions. Additionally, the participants reported a lack of training in palliative care and cultural diversity as another barrier in end of life discussions. An open line of communication between patients and physicians can determine the patient's definition of a good death and the measures that the patient would not wish to employ near the end of life. In discussions concerning end of life issues between physicians and patients' families, the physicians are often the initiators and dominant voice in these conversations.

The participants in the study reported that their cultural beliefs do not impose on the patient's decision-making process. The participants also reported the patient's cultural beliefs impeded discussions regarding hospice services in most of the cases in which hospice referrals were delayed. Physicians must develop a level of cultural sensitivity about the patient population served, as well as an increased awareness of the influence of culture in shaping patients' values, beliefs, and views regarding the world around them. The respondents stated they have adopted an analytic approach to healthcare decisions when they interact with patients. This analytic approach, however, does not foster a supportive relationship between patients and physicians. The development of culturally compatible systems within healthcare provides a framework for the multidisciplinary team to approach complex, yet culturally sensitive end of life decision-making processes (Cort, 2004; Meier et al., 2004).

Physician Perspectives on Culture

The physicians in this research study defined culture similarly, with nearly 86% defining it as some set of beliefs or behaviors resulting from individual upbringing within a society. The majority of the participants agreed that culture plays a role in an individual's decision-making process (57%); however, the participants equally perceived that culture does not play a role in their own decisions made as a physician for a patient (57%). In theme 2, the participants mentioned rather that the patients' cultural beliefs have a significant impact of the decisions and the acceptance or rejection of recommendations made by the physician (35.7%). According to these respondents, this impact of culture on the part of the patient can at times create disconnect between the patient and the patients' family and the physician.

The participants stated that comprehensive training in terms of cultures in the Mercer County, New Jersey area would enhance the patient-physician relationships. Respect for differences and nuances inherent within each culture allow the healthcare professional to provide cultural competent care. The physicians' cultural disconnect within their own clinical practice has created a sterile relationship in which patients have identified an emotional chasm. A delicate balance between analytical reasoning and cultural sensitivity within the patient-physician relationship would foster effective communication regarding end of life decision-making.

Physician Perspectives on Hospice Care

The third theme categorized by the analysis isolates the physicians' perspectives on hospice and hospice care. The physicians in this study unanimously defined hospice care as an option for care that includes comfort measures in a situation of limited life expectancy (100%). The majority of the participants agreed that hospice is generally accepted or embraced by their own culture (71.4%), with some even alluding to the fact that hospice care is handled by the immediate family in their own culture (21.4%), eliminating a conflict of physician beliefs and culture in recommending hospice care for their patients. Nearly 29% of the participants mentioned the dignity of the patient in terms of their right or choice to die and decide their own fate. Although some participants perceived the resistance or acceptance of hospice care to be from the patient (21.4%), some also noted reluctance in other physicians to recommend hospice care (14.3%). Additional studies revealed that most physicians cite late hospice referrals as a direct result of family reluctance to accept patient prognosis and that death was near (Chung, Essex, & Samson, 2008; Sanders, Burkett, Dickinson, & Tournier, 2004). Research by Teno et al. (2007) revealed that hospice referrals were appropriate; however, short hospice stays affected the quality of end of life care received. Transition from personal culture to organizational culture depends on the individual physician's medical training and acculturation into the healthcare system. Regulatory and healthcare policies provide guidelines for physician practice; however, it does not dictate the direction of clinical practice.

Communication with Patients

Within this particular theme, participants most commonly expressed that communication is significantly impacted by patient culture (14.3%). The other constituents in this theme received only one response (7%). With regard to these constituents, individual participants noted that having a similar culture as the patient can make communication easier and that having a different culture than the patient can make communication more difficult or frustrating for the physician. Only one participant gave direct examples of when a patient's culture created a conflict with letting the patient die (7%).

Interactions between physicians, patients, and their family vary based on established relationships, communication styles, and cultural beliefs (Kawaga-Singer & Blackhall, 2001). Barclay, Blackhall, and Tulsky's (2007) study revealed good communication skills result in better patient outcomes, increased patient satisfaction, and improved understanding of end of life options, including hospice. Cultural similarities between physicians and patients assist in the development of healthy relationships. Effective communication skills delve deeper than the immediate similarities found through cultural bonds. Participants reported the lack of training on effective communication skills hindered the initiation of sensitive discussions surrounding topics such as palliative care, end of life, and hospice.

The patient-physician relationship is fraught with boundary issues. Transference requires constant monitoring during communications in the patient-physician relationship while maintaining professional boundaries. Physicians are also susceptible to transference in the patient-physician communication process as their own cultural beliefs may influence the way in which a patient may view end of life decisions, thus having an effect on the way in which a patient and their family may have wished to be treated clinically (Vincent, 2001). Cultural transference may occur automatically and feel natural for patients to revert to behaviors previously experienced (Adams, Bader, & Horn, 2009). Barclay et al. (2007) found each individual brings his or her own cultural context to each encounter. The role of the physician is to recognize the impact the cultural beliefs may have on end of life communications and decision-making. The cultural dialogue between patient and physician requires the physician to examine the verbal and nonverbal subtext of each interaction without interjecting his or her own individual cultural beliefs. The lack of communication skills training within the medical and residency programs of the participants illustrates the emphasis on the scientific aspects of medicine while the psychosocial needs of the patient are not considered.

Physician Training and Experience

Over 21% of the respondents agreed that experience aids in the ability to perceive the right time to initiate the end of life discussion and recommendation of hospice care. An additional 14.3% acknowledged that it is difficult to know when to recommend hospice care, knowing that there is nothing left to offer the patient except hospice care. According to the participants, physicians are trained to treat patients and make them better. It is difficult for a physician to 'switch gears' and admit that there is nothing left to offer other than comfort. A few participants also mentioned that issues pertaining to death and dying is included in American medical curriculum, but not necessarily in foreign schools (14.3%).

The incorporation of culture competence, communication skills, and end of life discussions in medical school and residency curriculum would prepare physicians to initiate difficult dialogues with patients and their families (Cherlin et al., 2005; Reilly & Ring, 2004). Ongoing continuing education allows physicians to review communication skills and identify deficiencies in clinical practice. Koenig (1997) suggested cultural competence could enhance lines of communication and establish a relationship between the patient and physician in which discussions with regard to viable treatment options are framed in cultural and medical context. The implementation of end of life curriculum in medical schools and residency programs would provide physicians with the opportunity to explore their own feelings regarding death and dying (Hart, Skillman, Fordyce, Thompson, Hagoplan, & Konrad, 2007; Reilly & Ring, 2004; Taylor, Hammond, DiCarlo, Karabatso, & Deblieux, 2006; Ury, Arnold, & Tulsky, 2002;). A few participants expressed concern regarding the end of life curriculum in international medical schools. Aligning the medical school curriculum to address the disparities identified by the participants would provide uniformity within the profession.

SUMMARY OF FINDINGS

The physicians in this study unanimously defined hospice as a treatment option that includes comfort measures for terminally ill individuals with a life expectancy of six months or less. Although some participants perceived the resistance of the hospice referral to be from the patient, some also noted reluctance in other physicians to recommend hospice. The majority of the participants agreed that culture plays a role in an individual's decision-making process; however, the participants equally perceived that culture does not play a role in their own decisions made as a physician. Respondents expressed ease in communication with patients of similar cultural backgrounds compared to communication with individuals of different cultural backgrounds. The participants perceived this to be due to lack of training (communication skills) and knowledge (cultural competency).

RECOMMENDATIONS

The results of the study provide patients and allied health professionals with insights into the thought process of physicians with regard to culture and end of life issues. From the patient perspective, the results of this study provide a point of reference to draw upon when engaged in end of life discussions. The physician's cultural separation creates a disconnect when communicating with patients. The participants in this study identified cultural issues and communication barriers inherent in physicians-patient relationships.

The results of the study also provide a framework for allied health professionals such as social workers, nurse case managers, and patient navigators. The physician participants' candid revelations that individual cultural beliefs seldom influence decision-making offer a glimpse into a subculture of medicine not usually afforded to non-physicians. Discharge planning relies on the collaboration between the physician and allied health professionals to provide a smooth transition for the patient at the end of treatment. Communication plays a vital role in streamlining this process. The opportunity exists for social workers to assist physicians with improving end of life discussions with patients.

The Regulatory Focus Theory differentiates the ways in which people approach pleasure and avoid painful situations (Higgins, 1997). The theory states that individuals have two basic yet distinct self-regulation systems: one regulates achievements and individual focus on goals (promotion-focused), while the other regulates adherence to established rules and avoidance of punishment (prevention-focused). To understand the emotional and social processes of an individual and the social environment in which they function, one must understand the context of the relationship between them and the continual influence that another individual, social system, and event may have on the operation of the other. The results of the study illustrate the participants' alignment with prevention-focused individuals. Physicians are trained to adjust their practice to accommodate various regulatory and governing bodies. Over time, the physicians become less promotion focused and place more emphasis on prevention focus to remain in compliance with various regulatory bodies. The regulatory focus theory recognizes the individuality of each leader as the unique component that influences his or her motivation to lead and his or her ability to lead effectively.

The framework of this research study was to understand the cultural beliefs of physicians and end of life decision-making process. The conclusions derived from this study suggest that an initial effort at understanding the perceptions of cultural beliefs of physicians in end of life decision-making may lead to an increased awareness of the cultural beliefs of their patients and need for improved education about end of life for both the physicians and patients. Central to the physician leader's ability to connect with his or her patient during end of life situations is communication skills.

The physicians acknowledged that their education and residency varied based on where they received their medical training. Eight of the fourteen participants identified an "unwritten curriculum" within medical schools that encouraged an analytical, not cultural, perspective when engaged in the physician-patient relationship. One physician described the experience as 'cultural separation', the separation of an individual from his or her cultural belief to that of the health care culture. Acculturation into the health care community occurs over the course of the physician's training and includes the introduction of medical terminology and lingo, which further serves to separate the physician from the patient. The results of the study may influence the curriculum of medical schools and residency programs and health care policies with regard to communication skills, end of life discussions, and hospice.

CONCLUSION

The participants demonstrated detachment from their cultural beliefs when discussing their medical decision-making and end of life discussions with patients. The cultural separation described by the participants further illustrates the emotional detachment found in the physician's relationships with patients, allied health professionals, and health care administrators. The results of this study filled a gap in previous literature by demonstrating that physicians perceive there is a lack of knowledge in communication skills that hinder end of life discussions. The administrators of health care systems who focus on physician-patient communication, ongoing physician education and development, and cultural competency throughout the organization have the potential to create a safe environment where physicians, allied health professionals, and patients will benefit.

End of life decision-making continues to be met with difficult conversations due to cultural differences and lack of communication skills. Additional research would be useful in further assessing the perceptions and awareness of hospice, physician-patient relationships, and end of life curriculum within medical schools and residency programs. Repetition of this study could occur and involve interviewing physicians in similar geographical locations throughout the United States.

References

Adams, C., Bader, J., & Horn, K. (2009). Timing of hospice referral: Assessing satisfaction while the patient receives hospice services. *Home Health Care Management & Practice, 21*(2), 109–116.

American Heritage Dictionary (3rd ed.). (1994). New York: Dell Publishing.

Barclay, J., Blackhall, L., & Tulsky, J. (2007). Communication strategies and cultural issues in the delivery of

bad news. *Journal of Palliative Medicine, 10*(4), 958–977.

Beauchamp, T., & Childress, J. (1994). *Principles of biomedical ethics (4th ed.).* Oxford: Oxford University Press.

Casarett, D., & Quill, T. (2007). I'm not ready for hospice: Strategies for timely and effective hospice discussions. *Annals of Internal Medicine, 146*(6), 443–451.

Cherlin, E., Fried, T., Prigerson, H., Schulman-Green, D., Johnson-Hurzeler, R., & Bradley, E. (2005). Communication between physicians and family caregivers about care at the end of life:

When do discussions occur and what is said. *Journal of Palliative Medicine, 8*(6), 1176–1185.

Chung, K., Essex, E., & Samson, L. (2008). Ethnic variation in timing of hospice referral: Does having no informal caregiver matter? *Journal of Palliative Medicine, 11*(3), 484–491.

Cort, M. (2004). Cultural mistrust and use of hospice care: Challenges and remedies. *Journal of Palliative Care, 7*(1), 63–71.

Devore, W., & Schlesinger, E. (1995). *Ethnic-sensitive social work practice. (4th ed.).* Boston: Allyn Bacon.

Gauthier, D. (2005). Decision-making near the end of life. *Journal of Hospice & Palliative Nursing, 7*(2), 82–90.

Hart, L., Skillman, S., Fordyce, M., Thompson, M., Hagoplan, A., & Konrad, T. (2007). International medical graduate physicians in the United States: Changes since 1981. *Health Affairs, 26*(4), 1159–1169.

Hern, H., Koenig, B., Moore, L., & Marshall, P. (1998). The difference that culture can make in end of life. *Cambridge Quarterly of Healthcare, 7*(1), 27–40.

Hickman, S. (2002). Improving communication near the end of life. *American Behavioral Scientist, 46*(2), 252–267.

Higgins, E. (1997). Beyond pleasure and pain. *American Psychologist, 52*(12), 1280–1300.

Kawaga-Singer, M., & Blackhall, L. (2001). Negotiating cross-cultural issues at the end of life. *JAMA, 286*(23), 2993–3001.

Koenig, B. (1997). Cultural diversity in decision-making about care at the end of life. Retrieved January 22, 2007 from www.nap.edu/readingroom/books/approaching/appe.html

Lapine, A., Wang-Cheng, R., Goldstein, M., Nooney, A., Lamb, G., & Derse, A. (2001).

When cultures clash: Physician, patient, and family wishes in truth disclosure for dying patients. *Journal of Palliative Medicine, 4*(4), 475–480.

Larkin, P., & Schotsmans, P. (2007). Transition towards end of life in palliative care: an exploration of its meaning for advanced cancer patients in Europe. *Journal of Palliative Care, 23*(2), 69–79.

Lobar, S., Youngblut, J., & Brooten, D. (2006). Cross-cultural beliefs, ceremonies, and rituals surrounding death of a loved one. *Pediatric Nursing, 32*(1), 44–50.

Matzo, M. (2004). Palliative care: Prognostication and the chronically ill. *American Journal of Nursing, 104*(9), 40–49.

Meier, D., Thar, W., Jordan, A. Goldhirschm S., Siu, A., & Morrison, R. (2004).

Integrating case management and palliative care. *Journal of Palliative Medicine, 7*(1), 119–134.

Morrison, R., Maroney-Galin, C., Kralovec, P., & Meier, D. (2005). The growth of palliative care programs in United States Hospitals. *Journal of Palliative Medicine, 8*(6), 1127–1134.

Moustakas, C. (1994). *Phenomenological research methods.* Thousand Oaks: Sage.

O'Gorman, S. (1998). Death and dying in contemporary society: An evaluation of current attitudes and the rituals associated with death and dying and their relevance to recent understandings of health and healing. *Journal of Advanced Nursing, 27,* 1127–1135.

Reilly, J., & Ring, J. (2004). An end of life curriculum: Empowering the resident, patient, and family. *Journal of Palliative Medicine, 7*(1), 55–62.

Ruhnke, G., Wilson, S., Akamatsu, T., Kinoue, T., Takashima, Y., Goldstein, M., Koeing, B., Hornberger, B., & Raffin, T. (2000). Ethical decision-making and autonomy: A comparison of physicians and patients in Japan & the United States. *Chest, 118,* 1172–1182.

Sanders, B., Burkett, T., Dickinson, G., & Tournier, R. (2004). Hospice referral decisions: The role of physicians. *American Journal of Hospice & Palliative Medicine, 21*(3), 196–202.

Stroud, R. (2002). The withdrawal of life support in adult intensive care: An evaluative review of the literature. *Nursing in Critical Care, 7*(4), 176–184.

Taylor, L., Hammond, J., DiCarlo, R., Karabatsos, G., & Deblieux, P. (2006). A student-initiated elective on end-of-life care: A unique perspective. *Journal of Palliative Medicine,* 86–91.

Teno, J., Shu, J., Casarett, D., Spence, C., Rhodes, R., & Conner, S. (2007). Timing of referral to hospice and quality of care: Length of stay and bereaved family members' perception of the timing of hospice referral. *Journal of Pain and Symptom Management, 34*(2), 120–125.

Ury, W., Arnold, R., & Tulsky, J. (2002). Palliative care curriculum development: A model for a content and process-based approach. *Journal of Palliative Medicine, 5*(4), 539–548.

Vincent, J. (2001). Cultural differences in end of life care. *Critical Care Medicine, 29*(2), N52–N55.

Walker, W. (2007). Ethical considerations in phenomenological research. *Nurse Researcher, 14*(3), 36–45.

About the Author

New York native Dr. Karleen Yapp holds several nationally accredited degrees: a Bachelor of Arts (BA) from the University of Florida; a Master of Social Work (MSW) from Fordham University; and a Doctorate of Health Administration (DHA) from the University of Phoenix School of Advanced Studies.

Dr. Karleen is a health care professional with 10 years of experience focused on oncology services and supporting geriatric population within the mental health environment. Dr. Karleen also offers expertise in program development and management, clinical research, case management, service delivery, client education, and staff development.

Dr. Karleen is a member of the National Association of Social Workers and Zeta Phi Beta Sorority.

To reach Dr. Karleen Yapp for more information on any of these topics, please email: drkarleenyapp@consultant.com.

CHAPTER 4

Behavioral Integrity: The Precursor to Ethical Leadership

Dr. Cynthia Ann Roundy

E thics transcends the basics found within organizational policies, codes of conduct, the teachings in business/management schools, and even current legislation. Without a strong understanding of ethics, the moral essence of its nature and the applicability to human behaviors, organizations and society as a whole will continue to battle inequities, injustice, and dishonest leadership.

> But ethics isn't simply about all these things—right and wrong, good and bad, virtue and vice, benefit and harm, propriety and impropriety. So too is it about principle—fixed, universal rules of right conduct that are contingent on neither time, nor culture nor circumstance. (Foster, 2003, p. 5)

The creation of a strong ethically based environment is not an easy endeavor and it becomes literally impossible without the appropriate leader.

What is it then that we need to look for in our quest for ethical leadership? Is it simply a matter of searching for an individual of high intellect? Is it a matter of choosing leaders based upon the schools that they attended, their societal status, or their physical traits? Do they need to look like a leader and behave authoritatively? Do the answers to these questions lead us down a slippery slope of discrimination that has yet to be defined as illegal? The study of ethics provides us with deeper insights and wiser judgments into determining who is best to establish, emulate behaviors, and lead ethically based institutions.

> Nothing can be conceived in the world, or even out of it, which can be called good, without qualification, except a good will. Intelligence, wit, and other talents of the mind, however they may be named, or courage, resolution, perseverance, as qualities of temperament, are undoubtedly good and desirable in many respects; but these gifts of nature may also become extremely bad and mischievous if the will which is to make use of them, and which, therefore constitutes what is called *character,* is not good. (Immanuel Kant—Fundamental Principles of the Metaphysics of Morals as cited in Richardson, 2005, p. 7)

Many scholars have argued that it is the combination of *strategies, innovation, vision,* and *leadership* that determine the overall value to various stakeholders (Bate & Johnston Jr., 2005; Gelder, 2005). Major indicators related to organizational success include the role of leadership and the subsequent behaviors of the leader (Brown, 2003; Giblin & Amuso, 1997; Hood, 2003). Leadership is ultimately responsible for the vision, implementation, and support of organizational strategies. It is also the leader that is accountable for the creation of an organizational culture that either supports innovation or supports the status quo (Malloy & Agarwal, 2003). As such, the imperatives for building organizational environments that are open, diverse, knowledge infused, innovative, empowering, and ethically based are dependent upon the behavioral integrity of the leader. It is also the impact of the leader that drives the actions, loyalties, motivation, and behaviors of the followers. As asserted by Gelder (2005), the leader's role is about "creating the vision, structures, systems, trust and clarity that inspire people in the organization to achieve its strategy and apply their creativity to the things they do in their work" (p. 5). Mayfield and Mayfield (2004) further define the role of a leader as one who uses *motivating language* to guide, exhibit empathy, and provide meaning to subordinates. The leader, therefore, envisions the dream, sets the course, and drives followers to endorse the mission and emulate behaviors representative of that leader.

This chapter will examine the need for organizational and personal integrity within today's corporate climate. It will additionally confirm that the character of the leader is the primary power that both demonstrates and drives behaviors that will consequently result in transparent, honest, and equitable cultures. The approaches or strategies that leaders select may be indicative of their leadership styles and personal ethical convictions (Bass, 1990). This chapter will additionally examine a potential link between emotional intelligence and the behavioral integrity of the leader. The overall question that continues to be a matter of scholarly debate is "Who is best to lead?"

THE NEED FOR ORGANIZATIONAL INTEGRITY

A critical first step for every organization is to acknowledge the fact that unethical leadership and practices have infiltrated their domains. Illegal actions, poor strategies, and other improprieties have led to the demise of several giants in industry and the impact to employees and other stakeholders has been direct and deleterious. "According to the Association of Certified Fraud Examiners, U.S. companies lose roughly $400 billion dollars a year to internal fraud" (Cialdini, Petrova, & Goldstein, as cited in Richardson, 2005, p. 41). Beyond monetary losses was the loss of both reputation and confidence in big business and leaders that governed them. The communication and transparency of what has transpired in organizations such as Enron indicates a desperate need for different organizational strategies and leadership. "Companies without a moral compass are cast adrift or broken apart on the rocks" (Hatcher as cited in Richardson, 2005, p. 100). Control and eventual amelioration of unethical organizational practices and behaviors and the reinstatement of organizational integrity and high personal character needs to be the new directives of today's corporations.

Current State of Businesses

Organizations such as Enron, WorldCom, and Tyco once characterized as successful firms that had engaged in unethical practices, were led by unethical leaders, and suffered irreparable damages (Appelbaum, Deguire, & Lay, 2005; Giblin & Amuso, 1997). Perhaps the foundational lesson learned from the current state of organizational conditions is the importance of a renewed focus on ethical practices and the type of leaders that will best foster these principles (Stephenson, 2004). The current state of business issues is one that is clearly transitioning from closed cultures to ones that are more open and transparent in their dealings. It is reasonable to assume that this change in direction developed in the wake of recent corporate scandals. The focus is now on transformations in strategy and in the type of leaders that can best drive towards appropriate renewal.

Defining Organizational Integrity

Multiple descriptions of the concept of *integrity* exist. According to the Oxford dictionary, the term integrity is defined as "an unimpaired moral state, characterized by innocence, sinlessness, uprightness, honesty, and sincerity" (Oxford English Dictionary, 1989, as cited in Jacobs, 2004, p. 9). Integrity is additionally multidimensional where individuals become predisposed to act in ways that are morally appropriate and altruistic (Solomon, 1992, as cited in

Jacobs, 2004). Carson (1995) posited that integrity was an "unwavering commitment to acting for the benefit of others, standing up for those who are under attack, loyalty to people to whom we have committed ourselves, and acting honorably" (as cited in Jacobs, 2004, p. 215). In all, *integrity* is a necessary element towards the creation of an ethical organizational culture.

THE LEADER

The study of leadership and the quest for answers on how to identify the traits and characteristics of those that are most appropriate to lead has been a relentless pursuit (Higgs & Aitken, 2003). Although scholars have posited that multiple variables enter into the leadership equation, there remains a strong and rising support for utilizing emotional intelligence as an accurate predictor of leadership excellence (Langhorn, 2004). The following sections of this chapter provide a brief overview related to how emotional intelligence may impact leadership competencies, behavioral integrity and ethics, individual character, and overall leadership style.

Leadership and Emotional Intelligence

Emotional intelligence, with all of its many attributes, is a means by which leaders become self-aware, knowledgeable of their surroundings and circumstances, empathetic towards those in need, motivational towards organizational members, and ethically driven to both communicate and emulate corporate values (Abraham, 2004). Significant research on the impact of emotional intelligence on personal competencies, social competencies, ethics, and the ability to lead exists (Goleman, Boyatzis, & McKee, 2001). Emotional intelligence, as described by Brown (2003) is the ability to harness emotions and drive behavioral responses that are appropriate and will exact good outcomes. The behavioral choice is guided via the competencies of emotional intelligence and is affiliated with outcomes such as enhancing trust, building goodwill, improving morale, increasing loyalty, and improving performance (Macaleer & Shannon, 2002).

Several studies have indicated the value of emotional intelligence to leadership. Sy and Cote (2004) conducted a study with over 200 leaders from six major organizations and achieved results that supported the beneficial impact of emotional intelligence related to the ability to problem solve and further suggested that innovation, the ability to motivate others, and aptitude for information processing were impacted by these competencies. Ferris and Connell (2004) verified the value of emotionally intelligent leadership related to implementing change initiatives. This research conducted in a large public sector organization indicated that leaders with high emotional intelligence were better able to facilitate innovative organizational change. According to Ferris and Connell, changes driven by these leaders led to reduced cynicism and resistance by employees.

These studies suggest a general conclusion that specific traits, related to emotional intelligence, are those concomitant with behaviors manifested by ethical leadership practices. Goleman (1998) noted that an effective leader has a high level of emotional intelligence and without these competencies; an individual will never become a great leader. Further research may provide additional quantitative and qualitative data to clarify the benefits of emotional intelligence to the study of leadership.

Emotional Intelligence and Behavioral Integrity

According to Goleman (1998), several competencies associated with emotional intelligence manifest themselves through humanitarian and benevolent behaviors. These competencies include empathy, social awareness, conscientiousness, trustworthiness, honesty, teamwork, and visionary leadership (Cherniss & Goleman, 2001; Goleman). According to multiple studies conducted by Kouzes and Posner (2002), the trait recognized as most essential to leadership excellence was honesty, a competency of emotional intelligence. As such, emotional intelligence levels may act as indicators of a leader's behavioral integrity and overall character.

Leadership Styles and Behavioral Integrity

What leader can best promote the highest levels of organizational and personal behavioral integrity? Is there a specific leadership style that best meets these criteria? According to scholars, emotionally intelligent leaders have competencies that are associated with characteristics attributed to the transformational style of leadership (Bass, 1990; 1999). According to Bass (1999), the transformational leader "elevates the follower's level of maturity and ideals as well as concerns for achievement, self-actualization, and the well-being of others, the organization, and society" (p. 9). It is the value-centered, selfless, and ethically driven nature of the transformational style that sets it apart from others. Bass has also asserted that while an organization cannot effectively operate solely with a *task* or *relations* orientation, a balance of both has resulted in greater performance and an overall acceptance of the leader by others. The nature of the transformational leader is multidimensional and integrates elements of directive and participative leadership tendencies, ethics, and morality (Bass). The transformational style of leadership may potentially be most effective in creating and supporting organizational cultures that are innovative, empowering and ethically sound.

The Leader as a Change Agent

Based upon the required abilities of the change agent, leadership style may be a key indicator of successful and positive initiatives. Task oriented leaders, for example, most typically follow a style that has been defined as autocratic (Bass, 1990). The characteristics of the autocrat is one that literature suggests fundamentally lacks specific emotional intelligent competencies such as empathy, teamwork, motivation, building of bonds, vision, adaptability, catalyzing change, and inspirational leadership (Goleman, Boyatzis, & McKee, 2001). According to Bass, (1999), these characteristics, however, are those affiliated with transformational leadership. These leaders are best able to envision, evaluate, and ensure the 'need' for change. They are also most effective in communicating a purpose of the change or innovation to employees as a means of its justification (Fernandez & Rainey, 2006).

IMPACTING THE BEHAVIORAL INTEGRITY AND CHARACTER OF FOLLOWERS

It is essential that strong ethical cultures encompass values internalized by all organizational members. Organizational leaders must articulate, support, emulate, and enforce values, beliefs, and expected ethical behaviors (Giblin & Amuso, 1997; Stephenson, 2004). Many researchers assert that the *leader* sets the ethical tone relative to the organizational culture (Malloy & Agarwal, 2003). "For decades business ethics professors have been talking about how the moral tone of the organization is set at the top-and by the same logic-the immoral tone is also set at the top" (Carroll & Scherer, 2005, as cited in Richardson, 2005, p. 174).

Several studies have provided evidence that the leader directly influences the organizational culture and the behaviors of the followers. According to a study by Malloy and Agarwal (2003), results indicated that the behavior of leaders, their leadership styles, and their decision-making processes directly affected the member's perceptions of an ethical climate. Wilson (2003) evaluated the association between social dominance orientation (organizational ranking) and ethical perceptions. Results indicated that as social dominance orientation increased, ethical positioning decreased. Based on these findings, Wilson purported that individuals exhibiting high social-dominance orientation may seek to meet all organizational objectives regardless of the means. Such individuals would view issues related to ethics or morality as unimportant and actions toward goals would continue regardless of damages to employees or the organization (Wilson). A study by Hood (2003), analyzed the association between CEO values, leadership styles, and ethical practices. General findings indicated that ethics of the leader was a critical factor affecting the culture within an organization. Social and morally based values of the leaders were directly correlated with ethical practices within the firms. Results also indicated that transformational leaders were significantly more supportive of the establishment and endorsement of ethical mission statements (Hood, 2003).

Trevino, Weaver, Gibson, and Toffler determined an employees' view of an organizational culture directly influences their loyalty and performance within that construct (Hartman, 2005). Injustices handled in 'soft' or ineffective ways could lead to increased employee cynicism within the organization. These perceptions would additionally challenge the process to implement an ethically sound organizational construct.

These research studies suggest a conclusion that leaders with behavioral integrity and high moral character will aggressively drive towards ethically sound organizational cultures. They are individuals that aspire to creating environments that are empowering, open, innovative, motivating, and just. These leaders are additionally more dedicated to the values and code of ethics of the organization and are willing to self-sacrifice in order to seek the greater good for employees and the organization alike.

STRATEGIES OF ETHICALLY BASED LEADERS

Leaders with high standards of organizational and behavioral integrity would be strong advocates for the creation of business governance plans. The Institute of Business Ethics recommends that every organization prepare a Code of Ethics and Conduct to establish a standard set of values and expectations for all employees. Hartman (2005) suggests that organizations prominently display their documents in public areas within the organization and conduct training on the codes. In addition, implementation and adherence to the code is of the utmost importance. Employee accountability, at all ranks, would need to meet codes of ethics and mechanisms developed to deal with non-compliance should exist (Hartman, 2005).

Another strategy that focuses upon stages of ethical development is provided by Coleman (2000). This scholar provides six levels of ethical progress within an organization that are identified as: (1) commitment, (2) formulation, (3) action and feedback, (4) reevaluation, and, (5) total ethical integration (Coleman, 2000, as cited in Rossouw & Vuuren, 2003). These steps illustrate a slower process that is meant to ingrain concepts of ethics into the organizational culture over a period of time. The preceding strategies emphasize the importance of change and innovation. In addition, each approach focuses upon essential ethical underpinnings required within today's organizations. Clearly, these strategies establish the basis for both organizational integrity and behavioral integrity for those within these cultures.

Ethical Leaders and Leading Beyond the Obvious

Research and continued knowledge enhancement for the purpose of societal good may be critical for the amelioration of organizational problems such as discrimination and fraud that may be born of ignorance, prejudice, and hypocrisy. Kincheloe and McLaren (1994) noted:

> Critical research can be best understood in the context of empowerment of individuals. Inquiry that aspires to the name critical must be connected to an attempt to confront the injustice of a particular society or sphere within the society. Research thus becomes a transformative endeavor unembarrassed by the label "political" and unafraid to consummate a relationship with an emancipatory consciousness. (p. 140)

Ethical leaders who are willing to gain new knowledge emerging from the study of workplace and societal issues may serve as needed change agents to drive toward reformations related to organizational problems. Bass (1990) provided the following insight into the expansion and optimization of the leadership role that may potentially address organizational problems such as workplace bullying, injustice, inequitable treatment, and covert destructive activities, in advance of legal requirements:

> It is influence over and above what is typically invested in the role—influence beyond what is due to formal procedures, rules, and regulations. Thus, managers are leaders only when they take the opportunity to exert influence over activities beyond what has been prescribed as their role requirements. (p. 14)

Leaders that aspire to meet objectives of an organization as well as drive towards a broadened moral purpose can strengthen the moral aptitude within that environment. These leaders additionally may also break down status quo barriers and subsequently lead in a manner that continues to optimize and sustain organizational and individual integrity.

CONCLUSION

This chapter consists of discussions surrounding ethical and moral schemata of an organization. The vision of the leader and the behaviors and standards emulated by that leader establishes the ethical compass of that construct. Kouzes and Posner (2002) quantitatively established that the credibility and integrity of the leader affects the bottom line of organizations. By effectively addressing the challenges presented by revelations of unethical leaders and organizational practices, corporations can begin the process of implementing innovative change initiatives with a direct focus on leadership, governance plans and regaining trust of the American public. Taken to its most transcendental level, the Bible additionally provides guidance to leaders that resonates the themes associated with the righteous leader.

> Hearken, you who are in power over the multitude and lord it over throngs of peoples! Because authority was given you by the Lord and sovereignty by the most high, who shall probe your works and scrutinize your counsels! Because, though you were ministers of his kingdom, you judged not rightly, and did not keep the law, or walk according to the will of God. Terribly and swiftly shall he come against you, because judgment is stern for the exalted—for the lowly may be pardoned out of mercy but the mighty shall be mightily put to the test. For the lord of all shows no partiality, nor does he fear greatness. Because he himself made the great as well as the small, and he provides for all alike; but for those in power a rigorous scrutiny impends. (Wisdom 6: 2–3)

The links discovered between behavioral integrity, emotional intelligence, transformational leadership, and ethics provide many insights into answering the question of who is best to establish and lead an ethically based organization. Multiple research studies as well as powerful Biblical messages further endorse the appropriate course of action if the scale of justice is to tilt in the direction of ethical discipline and justice. This transformation will undoubtedly evoke challengers and a multitude of obstacles, not the least being the defiance of unethical leaders whose desires it is to remain in positions of ultimate power.

References

Abraham, R. (2004). Emotional competence as an antecedent to performance: A contingency framework. *Genetic, Social, and General Psychology Monographs, 130*(2), 117. Retrieved from ProQuest database.

Appelbaum, S. H., Deguire, K. J., & Lay, M. (2005). The relationship of ethical climate to deviant workplace behaviour. *Corporate Governance, 5*(4), 43. Retrieved from ProQuest database.

Bass, B. M. (1990). *Handbook of leadership: Theory, research, & managerial applications* (3rd ed.). New York: Free Press.

Bass, B. M. (1999). Two decades of research and development in transformational leadership. *European Journal of Work and Organizational Psychology, 8,* 9–32. Retrieved from ProQuest database.

Bate, J. D., & Johnston Jr., R. E. (2005). Strategic frontiers: the starting point for innovative growth. *Strategy & Leadership, 33*(1), 12.

Brown, R. B. (2003). Emotions and behavior: Exercises in emotional intelligence. *Journal of Management Education, 27*(1), 122. Retrieved from ProQuest database.

Cherniss, C., & Goleman, D. (2001). *The emotionally intelligent workplace: How to select for, measure, and improve emotional intelligence in individuals, groups and organizations.* San Francisco: Jossey-Bass.

Denning, S. (2005). Why the best and brightest approaches don't solve the innovation dilemma, *Strategy & Leadership, 33*(1), 4.

Fernandez, S., & Rainey, H. G. (2006). Managing successful organizational change in the public sector. *Public Administration Review, 66*(2), 9.

Ferris, N., & Connell, J. (2004). Emotional intelligence in leaders: An antidote for cynicism towards change? *Strategic Change, 13*(2), 61. Retrieved from ProQuest database.

Gandossy, R., & Sonnenfeld, J. (2004). *Leadership and governance from the inside out.* Hoboken, NJ: John Wiley & Sons.

Giblin, E. J., & Amuso, L .E. (1997). Putting meaning into corporate values. *Business Forum, 22*(1), 14. Retrieved from ProQuest database.

Goleman, D. (1998). What makes a leader? *Harvard Business Review, 76*(6), 93. Retrieved from ProQuest database.

Goleman, D., Boyatzis, R.., & McKee, A. (2001). Primal leadership. *Harvard Business Review, 79*(11), 42.

Hartman, L. P. (1997). *Perspectives in business ethics.* New York: McGraw-Hill.

Higgs, M., & Aitken, P. (2003). Research note: An exploration of the relationship between emotional intelligence and leadership potential. *Journal of Managerial Psychology, 18*(7/8), 814. Retrieved from the ProQuest database.

Hood, J. N. (2003). The relationship of leadership style and CEO values to ethical practices. *Journal of Business Ethics, 43*(4), 263). Retrieved from ProQuest database.

Jacobs, D. C. (2004). A pragmatist approach to integrity in business ethics. *Journal of Management Inquiry, 13*(3), 215.

Kouzes, J. M., & Posner, B. Z. (2002). *The leadership challenge: How to get extraordinary things done in organizations* (3rd ed.). San Francisco: Jossey-Bass.

Langhorn, S. (2004). How emotional intelligence can improve management performance. *International Journal of Contemporary Hospitality Management, 16*(4/5), 220. Retrieved from ProQuest database.

Malloy, D. C., & Agarwal, J. (2003). Factors influencing ethical climate in a nonprofit organization: An empirical investigation. *International Journal of Nonprofit and Voluntary Sector Marketing, 8*(3), 224. Retrieved from ProQuest database.

Macaleer, W. D., & Shannon, J. B. (2002). Emotional intelligence: How does it affect leadership? *Employment Relations Today, 29*(3), 9. Retrieved from ProQuest database.

Mayfield, M., & Mayfield, J. (2004). The effects of leader communication on worker innovation. *American Business Review, 22*(2), 46.

Richardson, J. E. (2004). *Annual editions: Business ethics* (16th ed.). Dubuque, IA: McGraw-Hill/Dushkin.

Roundy, C. (2007). Workplace bullying: investigation the link to emotional intelligence. *Dissertations Abstracts International.* (UMI No. 33026250).

Stephenson, C. (2004, January/February). Rebuilding trust: The integral role of leadership in fostering values, honesty, and vision. *Ivey Business Journal Online.* Retrieved from ProQuest database.

Sy, T., & Cote, S. (2004). Emotional intelligence: A key ability to succeed in the matrix organization. *Journal of Management Development, 23,* 437. Retrieved from ProQuest database.

van Gelder, S. (2005). The new imperatives for global branding: Strategy, creativity and leadership. *Journal of Brand Management, 12*(5), 395.

About the Author

Upstate New York author Dr. Cynthia A. Roundy holds several nationally accredited degrees; a Bachelor of Science (BS) in Biology from Syracuse University, a Master of Science (MS) in Human Resource Management and Development from Chapman University; and a Doctorate of Management (DM) in Organizational Leadership from the University of Phoenix School of Advanced Studies.

Dr. Cynthia is unique in that she has had the privilege of her continuing employment with a Fortune 500 organization for over 25 years. Her *real life studies* of human behaviors, integrated with years of scholastic studies, have positioned her in an optimized manner to help others through her in-depth understanding of leadership and organizational ethics. Dr. Cynthia is an expert in the field of workplace bullying and is currently studying the impact of bullying in schools. She has conducted and continues to offer seminars on these topics in many venues.

Dr. Cynthia currently serves on the Board of Directors for the YWCA in Onondaga County and is the Vice President of S. Roundy LLC.

Additional published works include her dissertation: *Workplace Bullying: Investigating the Link to Emotional Intelligence* and *The Refractive Thinker: Vol. I: An Anthology of Doctoral Learners, Chapter 3.* Future offerings include her upcoming book in mid 2011 featuring key strategies for self-protection during hostile times.

To reach Dr. Cynthia Roundy for information on any of these topics, please e-mail: drcroundy@yahoo.com.

CHAPTER 5

How Understanding Impacts Ethics and Privacy

Dr. Tim Brueggemann

The reliance of organizations on the collection and storing of data for remaining competitive in the marketplace may have the potential to put the organization at significant risk. Organizations are sensitive to the protection of consumer data that is needed to perform the day-to-day operations by incorporating data security plans, disaster recovery plans, and risk mitigation plans; however, they may not be as concerned about protecting all of the data that is maintained on their systems. This data is known as Highly Sensitive Personally Identifiable Information (HSPII).

HSPII is defined as information which can be used to discern or to trace an individual's identity either alone or when combined with other information which is held in the public domain. Protection of HSPII data is essential to every company and requires a well developed set of rules and processes to be enforced by the Information Technology (IT) department. The rules and processes incorporated into a formal HSPII protection program must be understood by all IT workers in the organization. A HSPII protection program is best understood as a hybrid of a data security program and a privacy protection program. These programs can incorporate technology solutions that allow for encrypting of the HSPII data at a field level in the database, removal of HSPII data that is not essential to an application, establishing education programs for the IT worker, and specific instructions that relate to how HSPII data can be used by all employees of an organization.

Instant access to information and data is easier than ever to obtain, use, and share (Wen, Schwieger, & Gershuny, 2007). This can lead to more efficiency, but also can be dangerous if HSPII data that is collected is not properly protected from individuals or entities that do not have the need to access that information. This situation has the potential to increase the efficiency of both people and programs, but it can also negatively impact the protection of the HSPII from individuals or entities that do not have the need to access that information. There are many challenges that face an organization today, but no problem appears to be more important than the protection of the HSPII stored on the corporate systems and databases (Colson & King, 2001).

The integration of data is a challenge to all applications and organizations that need access to multiple data sources. This situation has become more prevalent as technology has grown. The vulnerabilities of these systems and the amount of data stored on these systems have the potential to affect every individual that has, or will have, their HSPII collected and used by an organization.

Lost or stolen laptops with employees' personal information, patients' medical records, students' educational records, or even the accidental mailings of information to other individuals or corporations have become commonly reported news stories. The amount and types of data collected by organizations today continues to grow. Of particular concern are policies and procedures that organizations incorporate to maintain the data.

New perspectives in organizational security have grown from the increased amount of government legislation and increased public awareness. Security does not naturally add a measureable value to the organizations IT systems. By contrast, an investment in the appropriate security levels reduces the potential risk of a loss to the organization. Selection of a suitable security policy and model is best if done earlier rather than later (Devanbu & Stubblebine, 2000). The primary challenge is to integrate the security requirements analysis into the analysis process of the IT organization. The vulnerabilities of an organization's systems, and the amount of data stored on these systems have the potential to affect every individual that has, or will have, their HSPII collected and stored on those systems.

Protecting HSPII data and creating an efficient and operational HSPII program combines the ethical actions of the IT professional, privacy, and data security. Webster and Dyar (2005) argue that organizations need to be informed on how to securely handle HSPII information. With the increase in identity theft across the nation the protection of the data must start with IT. Data security is an area that is one of the most studied, and often the area that is the most confused with a HSPII program. A well defined HSPII program must include policies, standards, and guidelines that are created and enforced by the IT staff.

The goal of this chapter is to highlight the importance of the IT professional having a sound understanding of HSPII programs. The remainder of the chapter is divided into the following areas: a discussion of privacy, ethical considerations, the methodology of the study, and the results of the study. The chapter concludes with a discussion of the findings.

PRIVACY

Privacy has always been an important issue and concern of people. The difficulty in defining privacy is that it is as much a concept as it is a thing, making it hard to define. Mary Gardiner Jones (1991), a prominent consumer advocate, contends that privacy rests upon the principle of individuals having the ability to control their personal information. The concern that arises is the ever increasing nature of electronic media. As a legal right privacy was defined by Samuel D. Warren and Louis D. Brandeis in 1890 as "the right to be let alone" (Kelly & Rowland, 2000). To date the legal right to privacy defined by Warren and Brandeis has not been enacted into law in the United States.

In the 1960s and 1970s Congress became increasingly concerned about the amount of data being stored on databases (Solove, 2003). Stemming from these concerns different legislations have been introduced in an effort to afford some type of privacy protection to the individual. Specific examples of these privacy protections include: (a) the Privacy Act of 1974 which gives individuals the right to access and correct information about themselves and restricts government agencies from disclosing any record to any other person or agency without written request and permission to do so, (b) the Health Insurance Portability and Accountability Act (HIPAA) governing the security and confidentiality of individually identifiable protected health information, and (c) the Family Education Rights Act safeguards the privacy of students by limiting the access and distribution of academic records (Solove, 2003).

Information Technology (IT) and the Internet have drastically changed how individuals can access information. Prior to this technology being available records were kept on microfiche or on paper and access to the information was more limited in scope. To get information people had to either physically go to the location the documents were stored or send a letter through the mail to request the documents. In the IT climate of today most of this information can be accessed quickly, from any location, and normally at little or no cost.

Etzioni (1999), like Warren and Brandeis, suggests that the unqualified right to be left alone and to maintain a sense of anonymity is one that is considered critical by society. These feelings of anonymity exceed the expectations of individuals when they enter required information on the Internet or share their personal information with others. Electronic commerce and increases in online technology have grown exponentially over the past two decades. This growth has provided many opportunities to increase organizational efficiencies and choices that are made by customers. These increases in technology also have presented an unparalleled rise of intrusions into Personally Identifiable Information (PII) and privacy (Kelly & Rowland, 2000). Often the breach of the person's privacy may not be known by or ever detected by the individual.

As technology continues to advance, more data is being collected without the majority of society knowing or understanding what is happening. Companies have the ability to examine the web logs on their servers to obtain information from customers, or prospective customers, visiting their web site. This information is involuntarily being given by the individual, and the individual is rarely informed that the information had been collected from them when they visited the web site (Kelly & Rowland, 2000). Livingston (2002) examined the Internet user's understanding of the safeguards for the collection of personal identifying information and how well the posted safeguards matched up with the guidelines developed by Organization for Economic Cooperation and Development (OECD) for information gathered during digital transformation. This study concluded that while most web sites had a privacy policy the diversity of the policies, and the interpretation level of the policies were widely varied among the sites studied.

Alderman and Kennedy (1997) stated "perhaps the scariest threat to privacy comes in the area known as informational privacy" (p. 323). Attacks on privacy occur in many areas: employment records, the internet, and from numerous government and corporate databases that contain HSPII data. The majority of the current discussions around privacy have a tendency to focus on the issues of what information is being collected about individuals and how that information is being distributed to others.

ETHICS FOR THE IT EMPLOYEE

Employees of a company play a large role in the ethical treatment and handling of the data stored on the company's systems. Regardless of the employee's job, every employee has the potential to come into contact with personally identifiable information. The Information Technology profession is at the forefront of ethical decision making, as this group of individuals is directly responsible for collecting, storing and writing the programs that store and use the data the organization has collected.

Just as computers and technology have taken a larger role in the organization, the IT professional has inherently taken on the responsibility to ensure the respectability of their profession. This respectability can only be obtained if the highest ethical and moral standards are practiced. "These standards are embodied in a Software Engineering Code of Ethics and Professional Practice, which has been recommended to the participating professional societies" (Gotterbarn, 1998, p. 26). This professional body of ethics will assist in the formulation of the rules the Information Technology profession must have, and utilize to be effective.

The Association for Computing Machinery (ACM) along with the Institute of Electrical and Electronics Engineers (IEEE) developed a code of conduct for sub specializations that fell under both of these professional societies (Gotterbarn, Miller, & Rogerson, 1997, p. 112). Having a code of conduct will not stop an employee from misusing the data they work with; it does however, provide guidelines, and expectations for the employee to follow. It is important to understand the code was never intended to be an all encompassing document or that its parts be used in justifying errors of omission or commission (Gotterbarn, Miller, & Rogerson, 1997). The code is a starting point to help software engineers in making ethical decisions. There will be instances where one set of standards may conflict with other sources. These situations allow for the software engineer to use ethical judgment to act in a manner that is the most consistent with the intent of the code of ethics.

For the majority of the day to day issues that a software engineer faces, codes like the ACM or IEEE code of ethics are not strictly enforced. There is no repercussion for failing to abide by the code, nor is there a requirement for members of this industry to join the ACM or IEEE. McFarland suggested in establishing a forum for discussing, judging and mediating ethical problems, and adjudicating conflicts to make members of the profession accountable (1990). Though there may indeed be a demand for such a forum, it can only complement, not replace the individual's internal ethical framework. This is especially true for daily work and research.

Ethical training must start at a bottom up level in order for it to be successful. Instituting a formal program to teach ethics, moral theories, and decision making has become essential. Teaching ethics to students is the first step to instill the desire and the resolve to be ethical (Schwarz, 2005). Those who teach, study, and practice in management information systems (MIS) are concerned about software piracy, access to confidential data, and use of company computers for an individual's private purposes (Benham & Jennifer, 1995). It is because of the concerns in these areas, that teaching students, and increasing the awareness on these subjects, will increase their ability to recognize and properly handle ethical issues when they arise.

The availability and the accessibility of information that the employee has access to in today's world has increased incrementally over the past number of years. The first step is to recognize that a problem exists or has the potential to exist. We often realize the existence of an ethical problem through damage that has been done or conflicts that may arise. Not all wrongs are ethical wrongs, but those that diminish the dignity, hopes, or rights of people have often an ethical problem at their core (Schwarz, 2005, p. 68). Understanding who the stakeholders are and what the possible options for actions are help to complement the decision making process for ethical problems.

While Schwarz advocates specific courses for students to learn and understand ethics in an information technology world, James Harris advocates teaching ethical standards as fixed portions of each course (2004, p. 47). In this way students are consistently reminded of the social and legal ramifications of misusing their knowledge. The main danger that occurs is that by not integrating ethics into undergraduate education, there is a concern that, the student will lack the ability to integrate ethics into their professional life (Greening, Kay, & Kummerfeld, 2004, p. 91).

While the best method of teaching ethics to computer science students is still under debate, the goal is to ensure that ethics is being taught. The overall outcome of a successful ethics training program will be two-fold: recognition of the need for professional and ethical behavior in software engineering, and a capacity for ethical reasoning (Schwarz, 2005, p. 70). This success will also have a positive effect on corporate entities. As more and more graduating computer science students have a better understanding of the ethical practices and policies that need to be applied to their chosen profession, the quality of professionals hired by these organizations will increase. These will not only help the organization in terms of the quality of the work produced, but will also help to reduce the potential of the misuse of their resources and the PII stored on their systems.

Study Methodology

The total population for this study was comprised of all IT workers employed by Fortune 500 companies within and outside of the

United States. It was unrealistic to access a population of this size for the purposes of this study; therefore, a convenience sample was taken from one large Fortune 500 company. In order to protect this company's identity, it will be referred to as Company A.

Company A has approximately 8,000 IT employees and a random sample of 10% of the staff was selected to participate in the study. The random sampling approach and the 10% sample were utilized to limit the impact on the organization's day-to-day business operations and at the same time provide a valid set of data for this study. A minimum response rate of 260, 32.5%, was necessary to represent the 800 employees selected to participate from Company A, and to meet the confidence level of 95% and the confidence interval of 5 for this study.

A listing of employees was provided from the Human Resources department. All employees that had an IT related job code were included in the initial set of potential respondents to this study. Only IT employees, full time or part time, of Company A regardless of their time with the company were eligible to participate in this study. Randomization was accomplished using a sequence generator from www.random.org/sequences. The sequence boundaries were determined for each job skill by finding the total number of employees in that skill code. The top 10% of numbers generated by the sequence generator were used to select the participants for this survey. An e-mail was sent to all of the randomly selected participants of the study. Reminder e-mails were sent out 1 week and 2 weeks after the initial e-mail to all participants thanking those that have already responded to the survey and requesting the non respondents to participate.

A self-administered Web-based survey was constructed for this study. The survey instrument allowed for data to be gathered and used to understand the extent to which IT professionals were aware of HSPII, and the data security provided by Company A's organizational HSPII program. To define the level of understanding the IT professional had on HSPII at their organization, questions on the survey were constructed to explore the following four areas: (a) knowledge of the HSPII program, (b) ascription to the technology used in the HSPII program, (c) belief in the ascription to technology, and (d) senior management role in the HSPII program.

Section one of the survey instrument gathered the demographic data. This data consisted of age, education level, time working in IT, time at current company, IT job function, and if the individual had direct reports. Section two of the survey captured HSPII program data. It consisted of 23 primary questions designed to determine the respondent's beliefs and understanding of the importance of a HSPII programs. Section three contained eight questions that related to the importance of information stored on an organization's systems. Gaining insight to the respondent's beliefs on data security has a direct impact on the HSPII program of an organization. The responses to the questions not only provide the respondent's view, but also present a unique perspective of the organization's HSPII program.

Six hypotheses were formed for this study. Hypotheses 1, 2, 3, 5, and 6 examined the impact of the IT employees' demographic factors and the understanding employees have toward Personally Identifiable Information Programs. Hypothesis 4 explored potential differences in understanding HSPII programs between employees that are responsible for direct reports and those who are not responsible for direct reports. The six resulting hypotheses of this research study are:

H_1: The time in the Information Technology field has a relationship to the Information Technology workers' understanding of Personally Identifiable Information Programs.

H_2: The education level of Information Technology employees has a relationship to their understanding of Personally Identifiable Information Programs.

H$_3$: The length of time with the company of Information Technology employees has a relationship to their understanding of Personally Identifiable Information Programs.

H$_4$: There is a difference in the understanding of Personally Identifiable Information Programs between those who have employees that report to them and those who do not have employees report to them.

H$_5$: The role of Information Technology employees has a relationship to their understanding of Personally Identifiable Information Programs.

H$_6$: The age of Information Technology employees has a relationship to their understanding of Personally Identifiable Information Programs.

Results of the Study

332 (41.5%) individuals participated in this study. Six demographic areas were examined: (a) length of time the individual has worked in the IT profession, (b) formal education level of the IT employees, (c) tenure with current company, (d) responsible for the managing of other employees, (e) IT Job Function, and (f) age. Figures 1–6 on the following pages, show the breakdown for each of these groups.

Hypothesis 1:
Time Working in Information Technology

The data from this study suggests that there is a correlation between how long an individual has worked in IT and the individual's understanding of HSPII programs. With a correlation significance of 0.111 there is sufficient evidence at the alpha level of significance, .05, to reject Hypothesis 1.

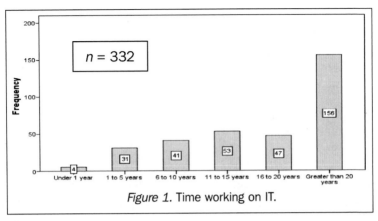

Figure 1. Time working on IT.

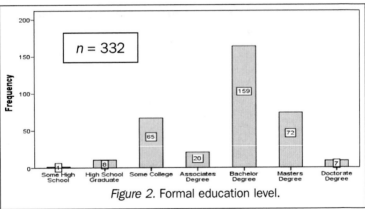

Figure 2. Formal education level.

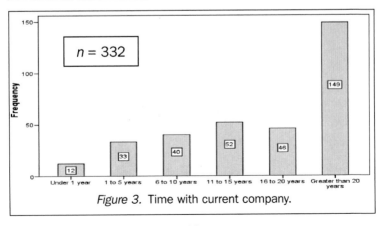

Figure 3. Time with current company.

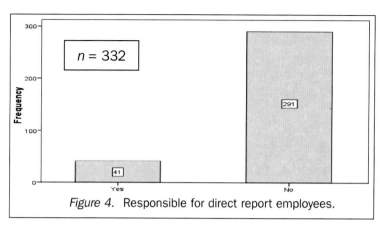

Figure 4. Responsible for direct report employees.

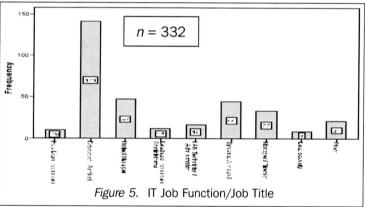

Figure 5. IT Job Function/Job Title

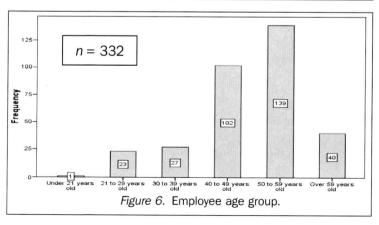

Figure 6. Employee age group.

Hypothesis 2:
Formal Education of IT and HSPII Understanding

The second demographic question asked for the highest level of formal education that the respondent had completed. This hypothesis tested the assumption that the more formal education an employee has completed the better his or her understanding of protecting HSPII will become. In comparing the highest level of education achieved by an employee with the understanding that the employee has of HSPII Programs there was an apparent correlation between the education level of the IT employee and the understanding of HSPII programs. With a correlation significance of 0.314 there is sufficient evidence at the alpha level, .05, to reject Hypothesis 2.

Hypothesis 3: Length of Time
with the Company and HSPII Understanding

This hypothesis examined the assumption that the longer an employee has been with the same company the better his or her understanding of protecting HSPII will become. Comparing the length of time with the company to the understanding that the employee has of HSPII programs a correlation between the length of time and employee has worked at the company and his / her understanding of HSPII programs was noted. With a correlation significance of 0.311 there is sufficient evidence at the alpha level of significance, .05, to reject Hypothesis 3.

Hypothesis 4: Employees Who Have
Direct Reports and HSPII Understanding

This hypothesis examined the assumption that employees of a company who have other employees reporting to them will have a better understanding of protecting HSPII data. Data in this study which suggests that IT employees that had other IT employees that were direct reports did have a better understanding of HSPII programs. With a correlation significance of 0.000 there is insufficient evidence at the alpha level of significance, .05, to reject Hypothesis 4.

Hypothesis 5:
Role of Employee and HSPII Understanding

This hypothesis examined the assumption that the role of IT employees, or job description, had a positive effect on the understanding of protecting PII data. The data collected in this study revealed that the Role of the IT employee did influence the Understanding of PII data protection. With a correlation significance of 0.049 there is insufficient evidence at the alpha level of significance, .05, to reject Hypothesis 5.

Hypothesis 6:
Age of Employee and HSPII Understanding

The final hypothesis examined the theory that the age of IT employees has a positive effect on the understanding of protecting PII data. The data collected in this study revealed that age of the IT employee did have an impact on the understanding of the organizational HSPII program. With a correlation significance of 0.002 there is insufficient evidence at the alpha level of significance, .05, to reject Hypothesis 6.

Summary of Study

This study focused on the IT professional's understanding of their professional and ethical responsibility in protecting HSPII data. Six hypotheses were tested to comprehend potential demographic factors as they relate to the construct of understanding. The demographic variables were age, formal education level, time with current company, time working in IT, job role, and whether the individual had any direct report employees.

The increased amount of electronic data that are produced and stored on organizational systems is a key HSPII and data security concern. While these data are not strictly stored on databases it still represents data that may have an impact on how organizations conduct their business. As the amount of data increases there is also an increase in the exposure to HSPII data that is incurred by the organization's IT professional.

Hypothesis 1 examined the assumption that the longer an employee has worked in the information technology profession the better his or her understanding of protecting HSPII would become. The data collected for this study suggest that understanding of PII data protection does not relate to the time an employee has worked in the IT profession. The data in this study coincide with literature that suggests the seniority of IT professionals has no impact on the security of the systems they support (Bowers, 2001). As IT systems continue to become more automated, increasing the IT employee's understanding of how to protect the data will reduce the risk to the security of the data on the organization's systems.

Hypothesis 2 examined the assumption that the more formal education an employee has completed the better his or her understanding of protecting PII data. Schwarz (2005) advocated specific courses for students to learn and understand his or her responsibilities in the IT environment. However, Robbins (2005) posited that the culture of the organization will have a greater influence on the IT professional. The data in this study support Robbins's claims. It was determined in this study that the understanding of PII data protection has no correlation to the formal education level achieved by the IT professional. The findings of this study could also be explained by the relative infancy of the IT field as an academic discipline.

Hypothesis 3 explored the length of time an employee has been with the same company and understanding of PII data protection. The data collected in this study determined that there is no association between understanding PII data protection as it relates to the time an employee has been with the company. Protection of personal information and creating a sound data protection program is an ongoing task within the IT organization (Solove, 2003). This study illustrates that understanding PIIP and data protection is an iterative process. All employees of the company, regardless of his or her tenure, must continually be exposed to data security and HSPII program processes.

Hypothesis 4 examined the assumption that employees of a company who have other employees reporting to them would have a better understanding of protecting PII data than those who did not have employees reporting to them. Understanding of PII data protection was affected by the employee having direct report employees assigned to them. The data collected in this study revealed that IT employees that had other IT employees that were direct reports did influence the Understanding of PII data protection. Eloff and Eloff (2003) contended that identification of the security needs should be the primary concern of management, and Freeman (2007) discussed Information Security from a perspective of understanding the requirements and the processes that the organization should take.

Hypothesis 5 scrutinized the assumption that the role of IT employees, or job description, had a positive effect on the understanding of protecting PII data. The data collected in this study revealed that the role of the IT employee did influence the understanding of PII data protection. Ward and Peppard (2002) posited that there are factors related to the role of the employee which have the potential to cause adverse effects on the understanding level of the organization's PIIP. The results of this study confirm Ward and Peppard's position. The highest demonstrated understanding level was found in the roles of manager/director with a mean score of 113.67, and data security specialists with a mean score of 112.50. While the lowest level of understanding out of the roles examined in this study was for the developer/analyst with a mean score of 98.87.

Hypothesis 6 examined the theory that the age of IT employees has a positive effect on the understanding of protecting PII data. The data collected in this study revealed that age of the IT employee did have an impact on the Understanding of PII data protection. Knowledge, Ascription to Technology, and Senior Management of PII data protection were also affected as compared to the IT employee age. Ascription to Technology-Belief for PII data protection revealed no influence when compared to the age of the IT employee.

CONCLUSION

This chapter explored the understanding level of HSPII programs by the IT professional. The IT professional is the primary custodian of the organization's data and, as such, their understanding of the HSPII program is an essential component of protecting HSPII data. As the technologies being used continue to improve, so too should the understanding of how to protect the data.

There were additional insights gained from this study. The first was with the demographic variable of individuals that had direct report employees. The data showed that those who had direct report employees scored higher in each category of the survey instrument, which would indicate a better understanding of the HSPII program. While it should be expected that this group have a solid understanding, it also raises the question of what the individuals who have direct report employees could do to increase the understanding of those that work for them.

The age group of the IT professional also provided some additional insight. The mean score for understanding in this demographic area rose for each of the age groups. This could be explained in many ways: experience in the IT profession, an increased focus on HSPII data as the individuals approach retirement, or personal experiences that relate to HSPII data loss. There was no additional exploration of this data finding in this study, but it would be a good follow on study.

The possibility of data loss continuously threatens the security and the availability of IT systems and IT resources. The HSPII program must be a reiterative process and must be ongoing for it to be of value. IT systems and applications need to continually be examined and evaluated to determine any new risks that may arise around HSPII data security. One of the risks, if not the primary risk to any HSPII program is a lack of understanding of the individuals most involved in protecting the data; the IT professional.

References

Alderman, E., & Kennedy, C. (1997). *The right to privacy.* New York: Vintage Books.

Benham, H. C., & Jennifer, L. W. (1995). A comparative study of ethical attitudes among MIS students and professionals. *SIGCPR Comput. Pers., 16*(3), 3–10.

Bowers, D. (2001). The Health insurance Portability and Accountability Act: Is it really all that bad? *Baylor University Medical Center Report, 14*(4), 347–348.

Colson, R. H., & King, C. G. (2001). Protecting online privacy. *CPA Journal, 71*(11), 66.

Devanbu, P. T., & Stubblebine, S. (2000). *Software engineering for security: a roadmap.* Paper presented at the Proceedings of the Conference on The Future of Software Engineering, Limerick, Ireland.

Eloff, J. H. P., & Eloff, M. (2003). *Information security management: a new paradigm.* Paper presented at the Proceedings of the 2003 annual research conference of the South African institute of computer scientists and information technologists on Enablement through technology.

Etzioni, A. (1999). *The limits of privacy.* New York: Basic Books.

Freeman, E. H. (2007). Holistic information security: ISO 27001 and due care. *Information Systems Security, 16*(5), 291–294.

Gotterbarn, D. (1998). *Raising the bar: a software engineering code of ethics and professional practice.* Paper presented at the Proceedings of the ethics and social impact component on Shaping policy in the information age, Washington, D.C., United States.

Gotterbarn, D., Miller, K., & Rogerson, S. (1997). Software engineering code of ethics. *Commun. ACM, 40*(11), 110–118.

Greening, T., Kay, J., & Kummerfeld, B. (2004). *Integrating ethical content into computing curricula.* Paper presented at the Proceedings of the sixth conference on Australasian computing education—Volume 30, Dunedin, New Zealand.

Harris, J. (2004). *Maintaining ethical standards for a computer security curriculum.* Paper presented at the Proceedings of the 1st annual conference on Information security curriculum development, Kennesaw, Georgia.

Jones, M. G. (1991). Privacy: A significant marketing issue for the 1990s. *Journal of Public Policy & Marketing, 10*(1), 133–148.

Kelly, E. P., & Rowland, H. C. (2000). Ethical and online privacy issues in electronic commerce. *Business Horizons, 43*(3), 3.

Livingston, S. N. (2002). *The protection of personal identifying information through posted Internet privacy policies.* (Doctoral dissertation, Capella University, 2007).

McFarland, M. C. (1990). Urgency of ethical Standards Intensifies in Computer Community. *IEEE Computer, 23*(3), 77–81.

Robbins, S. P. (2005). *Managing and organizing people.* Upper Saddle River, New Jersey: Prentice Hall.

Schwarz, T. S. J. (2005). *Teaching ethics and computer forensics: The Markkula center for applied ethics approach.* Paper presented at the Proceedings of the 2nd annual conference on Information security curriculum development, Kennesaw, Georgia.

Solove, D. J. (2003). Access and aggregation: Public records, privacy and the constitution. *Minnesota Law Review, 86*(6), 1137–1184.

Ward, J., & Peppard, J. (2002). *Strategic planning for information systems* (3rd ed.). Hoboken, NJ: Wiley & Sons Inc.

Webster, M. K., & Dyar, D. (2005). *Using a database-driven website to track sensitive data use.* Paper presented at the SIGUCCS, Monterey, California.

Wen, H. J., Schwieger, D., & Gershuny, P. (2007). Internet usage monitoring in the workplace: Its legal challenges and implementation strategies. *Information Systems Management, 24*(2), 185–196.

About the Author

Dr. Tim Brueggemann has earned several nationally accredited degrees; a Bachelor of Science (BS) from Webster University; a Master of Business Administration (MBA) from Lindenwood University; and a Doctorate of Philosophy (Ph.D.) in Information Technology Management from Capella University school of Business and Technology.

Dr. Tim has over 28 years of civilian and military experience in management as well as analysis, design, programming, testing and implementation of computer systems in both mainframe and networking environments. He currently is employed by a Fortune 500 company as a Chief IT Architect. He is proficient in multiple programming languages, project management, and team leadership skills.

Dr. Tim has been an Adjunct Professor for the School of Business and Entrepreneurship at Lindenwood University for the past 10 years. He teaches courses in Management of Information Systems., Systems Analysis & Design, Database Management, Web Site Design, Java, C#, Visual Basic, and Quantitative Methods.

Dr. Tim is also an active member of Phi Delta Theta Fraternity and is a Life Member of VFW Post 2866.

Additional works include his dissertation: *Is Information Technology Reducing Privacy: A Study of Protecting Personally Identifiable Information,* April 2009, *Understanding: The Key to Protecting Highly Sensitive Personally Identifiable Information,* April 2010.

To reach Dr. Tim Brueggemann for information on any of these topics, please e-mail: tjbrueg@sbcglobal.net.

CHAPTER 6

The Power of the River of Character in Organizations

Dr. Ramon L. Benedetto

Recent corporate scandals have raised interest within corporate boardrooms about organizational values and ethics (Van Lee, Fabish, & McGaw, 2005). As more company leaders recognize the need for stronger ethics programs in the aftermath of these scandals, values have emerged as important company qualities (Van Lee et al., 2005). Values are a major part of organizational culture (Chun, 2005), because values guide behaviors within organizations (Hitt, 1990).

Core values are important as foundational guides because of their intrinsic importance to the people within the organization (Argandoña, 2003; Collins & Porras, 1994). Although values affect views and behaviors, no consensus exists about the nature of values in business, which has implications for relations within a company as well as with external customers (Meglino & Ravlin, 1998). Without a consensus, the manner through which leaders instill, nurture, and reinforce values in the workplace is not clear (Hartman, 2006). Burns (1978) noted values are standards that specify criteria for guiding choices between or among alternatives. Brown, Trevino, and Harrison (2005) noted employees constantly look to leaders and others for guidance about ethical behavior. Thus, leaders play a critical role in setting the example and the standards through which ethical practices, ideals, and values are shown in the workplace (Brien, 1998).

Employees set their personal standards by what they see at the top of the organization; if a company officer crosses the line, employees believe breaches of standards are acceptable behaviors (Sims & Brinkmann, 2002). Unethical behavior leads to organizational inefficiency and ineffectiveness as well as missed opportunities, lost business, and damaged reputations (Neilson, Pasternack, & Mendes, 2004; Sims & Brinkmann, 2002). In contrast, leaders who use a positive, value-based approach to organizational ethics can influence an organizational culture that strengthens social integration and consistently achieves positive results, such as profitability and sustainability (Grojean, Resick, Dickson, & Smith, 2004).

Ethics differ from values and beliefs. Ethics are organizational rules of conduct that govern relations with others and stem from values that express beliefs about "the 'rightness' or 'wrongness' of certain behaviors" (Bruhn, 2005, p. 192). For an organization to be ethical, the organizational culture must reinforce ethical decision-making while also defining, teaching, and reinforcing organizational values (Bowen, 2004). Ethics and values are foundational elements of organizational culture because ethics are rules of conduct rooted in organizational values (Schein, 2004), are core to organizational culture, and affect how people treat others within the organization (Bowen, 2004). Badaracco (1998) noted how character formation flows continuously through one's life since a test of character arises every time a person chooses between two values. The choices made daily continually shape individual character and guide behaviors people display within various organizational settings (Badaracco, 1998).

Individual values stem from two sides of one's character. Performance character engages those intrapersonal values related to performing the best job possible whereas moral character relates interpersonal values with being the best person one can be toward others (Lickona & Davidson, 2005). Performance character reflects an internally directed concentration of personal elements of self-management through which individuals control their behaviors to focus on individual performance (Lickona & Davidson, 2005). Moral character reflects an externally directed perspective on interpersonal relationships with others through which individuals engage others in various social settings and through which parties receive mutual benefit with others (Lickona & Davidson, 2005). Because personal values are the heart of one's character, leaders must understand the critical relationships between performance and moral character and emotional intelligence that shape actions within organizational settings.

Individual values and character entwine with organizational culture because organizational decisions and actions reflect organizational values. Although some have questioned if organizations can have values since organizations do not have cognitive skills, organizational values have emerged as forces that can affect individual behaviors and organizational outcomes (Scott, 2002). Companies with apparent dysfunctional and negative behaviors often reflect the failure of leaders to align individual and organizational values (Neilson, Pasternack, & Mendes, 2004). Misalignment occurs when individual and organizational purposes differ. In contrast, leaders of high-performing businesses understand the complementary nature of individual and organizational values and the importance of aligning these values to achieve organizational survival and growth (Scott, 2002).

Although company codes of ethics intend to reduce negative and unethical behavior in the workplace (McCabe, Trevino, & Butterfield, 1996), company codes of ethics alone cannot inspire employees to act ethically or to achieve excellence (Arjoon, 2000). Organizational leaders bear the responsibility to define, establish, maintain, and nurture the right organizational culture within which right behaviors are made evident to employees, customers, suppliers, and other stakeholders consistently and constantly. Character development is continuous, thus organizational leaders must understand how character contributes to the normative side of organizational culture and success.

THE PROBLEM AND PURPOSE BEHIND THE STUDY

Although many business leaders fail to pay adequate attention to company culture and the values and motives related to ethical behavior, leaders bear the responsibility nonetheless for aligning personal performance with institutional expectations for ethical performance (Arjoon, 2000; Bragues, 2008; Dickson, Smith, Grojean, & Ehrhart, 2001). Too often, leaders speak about having an ethical culture without understanding the means and methods for operationalizing an ethical culture. This chapter describes an ethnographic study that explored how company leaders and employees nurtured an ethical culture of character, aligned performance with expectations, affirmed the values of the organization through character-based culture, and achieved extraordinary outcomes as a result of the culture.

The purpose of the ethnographic study was to explore the impact of a culture of character on the internal coherence of business practices in a northern Illinois company. A catering company served as the study subject because of the complexity of internal operations and the ability to observe all aspects of company operations within a tightly defined geographic area. The research explored how the characteristics of an ethical, character-based culture emerged, how the culture affected the ethical behavior and performance of company employees, and how the culture affected customer experiences and perceptions, including buying decisions.

RESEARCH METHODOLOGY AND DESIGN

According to Coulon (1995), ethnographic study examines practical activities, circumstances, and sociological reasoning as phenomena in their own ways. Ethnographies also seek to discern predictability and patterns of behaviors evident in daily routines of the people within a culture rather than describing all possible interactions within that culture (Angrosino, 2007). To understand these patterns, the study used context analysis and archival research, observations, interviews, and analysis of events and routines that spanned eight weeks of intense field research. Sixty interviews with employees, leaders, company founders, randomly selected customers, advisers, and suppliers provided personal perspectives on various aspects of company culture and performance. A validation survey with 17 employees, most of whom were not part of the interview cohort, reinforced findings that emerged from data analysis.

The ethnographic design examined all phases of company performance. Unlike ethnographic studies that focus on the internal culture of an organization, this study extended to observations of external events or daily deliveries where company employees served and interacted directly with external clients and customers. Intense analysis of company archives included customer feedback reports from several years that revealed how clients, customers, and suppliers viewed company culture as well as details of organizational history and culture, internal company communications, and numerous after-action reports.

Background

The study fell within six broad research areas: (a) business ethics and ethical business practices, (b) management and leadership practices, (c) virtue theory, (d) values, (e) organizational culture, and (f) character. Substantial literature exists on the topics of business ethics, ethical business practices, management and leadership practices, organizational culture, and the effect of leadership styles on organizational culture. Despite the scarcity of literature related to organizational character, Birnholtz, Cohen, and Hoch (2007) and McFarland

(2008) defined organizational character, but only the former distinguished organizational character from organizational culture.

The literature revealed key lessons about the qualities of a 21st century leader. First, the leader must be a person of strong character with exceptional emotional and cultural intelligence to face the challenges of globalization, rapid technological advancements, and diverse workforces (Chowdhury, 2003; Goleman, 1995; Kotter, 1996). Second, virtue in individual leaders and virtuous organizational leadership hinge on moral philosophy, positive psychology, Aristotelian ethics, and civility (Cameron, 2003; Carter, 1998). Third, virtues serve as the foundation of good character and strong organizational performance (Cameron, 2006).

SUMMARY OF THE RESEARCH AND CRITICAL FINDINGS

The ethnographic study found seven core elements that form character-based culture and guide individual and corporate performance. An 'artifact' is defined as a physical or visible object that represents cultural characteristics (Benedetto, 2009). The following paragraphs summarize the four artifacts and three practices at the core of character-based culture.

ARTIFACTS

Core Values

Core values were the central artifact within a culture of character and underpinned all facets of the company. Core values provided a commonality of purpose and formed the foundation of the organizational belief system and the decision-making process. Rather than being driven from the top, employees within the company developed the set of core values, which made the values easier to follow and enforce.

Critical Finding: Core values are Central to the Culture of Character

The primary core value of the company was to always do what is moral, ethical, and legal, which reflected a foundation in moral management and conformed behaviors to "a high standard of ethical, or right behavior" (Carroll, 2000, p. 39). The seven core company values defined organizational character through which company employees demonstrated the corporate identity of the company as well as the character of individuals representing the company (Hartman, 2006).

The company value of treating others with respect reflected the sixth core value of a fully functioning organization defined by Margulies and Raia (1994), which is to treat each human being as a person with a complex set of needs. The six values Margulies and Raia (1994) identified for fully functioning organizations were evident within the company, including opportunities for employees to influence the ways in which they identified with their work, the company, and the environment. By living the company core values, employees embodied the business as a social institution with moral power (McMahon, 1991).

Visionary Servant Leadership

Greenleaf (1977) stated, "The servant leader is servant first"(p. 27) meaning one must make conscious choices to serve the common good and to lead others to do the same. Natural servants are inclined to persevere because their highest priority rests with serving the needs of others, in contrast to someone who chooses to lead because of a prompting of conscience or feeling compelled to conform to a normative standard (Greenleaf, 1977). The founders of the company created the catering business in response to customers who were impressed with the quality, quantity, and service in their former restaurant business, thus, the company's servant mentality spanned nearly 30 years.

Critical Finding: Visionary Servant Leadership Guides the Character-based Culture

Founders and executives demonstrated visionary servant leadership, which guided the evolution of the company and sustained company growth. Co-leadership existed among executives, and shared leadership throughout the company reflected high moral principles. Humility was a common attribute of the CEO and other senior leaders, which set the example for employees as they reflected servant leadership in their interactions with external customers.

Although the CEO focused the team on "a common purpose toward the right objectives" (Greenleaf, 1977, p. 80), other founders played equally significant roles as co-leaders and "outstanding adjuncts" (Heenan & Bennis, 1999, p. 10) who reinforced the culture through their unique leadership qualities and practices. The CEO was the visionary conceptualizer, the chief operating officer ensured effective execution of the master plan, and the chief procurement officer integrated critical elements of the supply chain to support company goals. All three leaders used emotional intelligence in guiding others, with the authoritative and coaching leadership styles being most evident amongst leaders (Goleman, 2000).

Well-defined Organizational Purpose

Employees at every level of the company used a well-defined organizational purpose to guide their decisions and actions. Character-defining moments throughout the company's history had shaped and aligned the purpose with the core competences of the company.

The purpose reflected what the company could do exceptionally well while avoiding areas that interfered with the core purpose. The adherence of employee decisions with the core purpose contributed to company success.

Critical Finding: Organizational Purpose Guides Decision-making

The combined efforts of founders, leaders, employees, and advisers defined an "enduring character" of the organization that remained "consistent through time" and transcended changes in "product and market life cycle, technological breakthroughs, management fads, and individual leaders" (Collins & Porras, 1994, p. 221). The core ideology served as the 'bonding glue' that held the company together regardless of the challenge; this ideology was evident in the ways employees tested decisions against the values and business philosophy (Collins & Porras, 1994, p. 221). Employees had a long-term perspective based on perseverance, thrift, and a personal willingness to subordinate oneself to a broader purpose (Hofstede & Hofstede, 2005). Company leaders established a higher purpose of service excellence that transcended merely maximizing wealth or profit (Hamel, 2009).

An Excellence-centric Business Model and Commitment to Becoming a Great Company

Three years prior to the study, employees had unanimously adopted a 'Good to Great' philosophy (Collins, 2001). This philosophy, along with the seven core values, was physically visible to employees and visitors in the form of oversized placards strategically placed throughout the company. Employees reinforced the business model in formal meetings by reciting the philosophy and values, confronting the brutal facts and knowledge gaps with integrity, sincerity, and authenticity, and committing their actions to continuous improvement and service excellence. Company leaders appreciated employees as sources of corporate intelligence, but more important, employees consistently reflected a culture of discipline as they coordinated actions between functions. Company leaders tapped the talents and knowledge of a multidisciplinary Advisory Board that reviewed company operations periodically and gave recommendations to create best practices internally.

Critical Finding: Leaders Sustain Growth with a Good to Great Business Model

The business model embodied a culture of discipline that extended to the three value disciplines of market leadership: operational excellence, product leadership, and customer intimacy (Collins, 2001; Treacy & Wiersema, 1995). The company exercised customer intimacy by delivering "superior customer value" (Treacy & Wiersema, 1993, p. 84) and excelled in operations by giving clients reliable service at competitive prices.). Client and customer feedback reflected extremely high satisfaction with the quality and variety of foods produced by the company, the timeliness of delivery, and the professionalism, courtesy, enthusiasm, and friendliness of employees in all company functions.

Company leaders had an exceptional intuitive sense about business, including knowing when they needed outside help. By using an advisory board, company founders erected 'scaffolding' that "enabled the company to get to the next level of performance" (McFarland, 2008, p. 147). Advisory board members contributed fresh ideas and helped leaders avoid attempts to reinvent the wheel (McFarland, 2008). The critical contribution of advisers to big picture thinking was their ability to help leaders see connections to broader issues and events occurring in other industries (Mitroff, 2004).

Core Practices: Hiring for Character

Company success stemmed from the core practice of hiring for character. Rather than rely on an external training program, leaders taught character through their example, actions, personal discussions, and continual focus on the application of company core values. Employees eagerly and readily adapted to operational changes and showed considerable flexibility in performing multiple roles because they were already aligned with company core values through the selection process that recognized their innate character traits. Employees believed that hiring for character aligned the right people with the company and helped to reduce internal conflict because employees were focused on obtaining mutual goals.

Critical Finding: Hiring for Character Sustains Profitability

Beinhocker, Davis, and Mendonca (2009) noted leaders must regain trust by looking beyond shareholder value and include the concerns of other stakeholders such as employees, customers, and communities. Human resource practices reflected this trust between employees and their leaders. O'Toole and Bennis (2009) noted successful companies will be measured by the extent "to which executives create organizations that are economically, ethically, and socially sustainable [and where] a culture of candor" (p. 56) exists, features that already exist within the company and have led to success. The company's significant success and many awards over nearly 20 years of operation reinforced the merits of values-based leadership and hiring employees for their character.

Commitment to Service Excellence

Commitment to service excellence permeated all areas of the company and organizational performance. All employees knew excellence in customer service depended upon their conscientiousness as Level 1 highly capable individuals as well as their ability to work effectively with others as Level 2 contributing team members (Collins, 2001). Excellence extended to how employees used and relied upon information technology throughout the organization to share and manage knowledge.

Critical Finding: Commitment to Service Excellence Permeates All Activity

The team concept was the underlying organizational structure and the critical element through which employees achieved company objectives. Figure 1, opposite, presents the organizational structure through which leaders and employees integrated strategic leadership, organizational learning and knowledge, and effective execution to achieve performance excellence and competitive dominance (Latham & Vinyard, 2005; Tang & Bauer, 1995). Leaders eliminated conflict within the company through interdependent and integrated teams.

The commitment to service excellence grew out of the quality philosophy founders learned through their father and their business model that emphasized the culture of discipline as a core value and operational strategy. Most important, the founders understood service management, which is "a total organizational approach that makes quality in service, as perceived by the customer, the number one driving force for the operation of the business" (Albrecht, 1988, p. 20). Figure 1 reflects a servant leadership mentality where leaders serve others in the company who directly serve the client. Having senior leaders on the bottom of the structure rather than the top

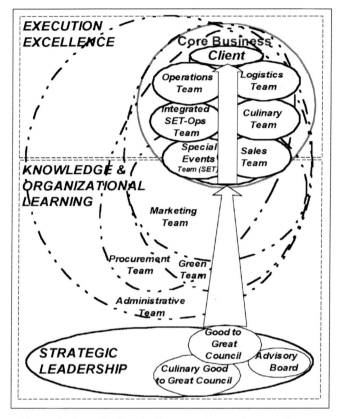

Figure 1: Organizational alignment for service excellence.

reflects the service model advocated by Albrecht (1988). Albrecht (1988) stated excellent service companies had employees who put customers and quality first, had "a 'whatever it takes' attitude" (p. 40) and saw managers as helpers and supporters.

Commitment to Lifelong Learning

Employees demonstrated a company-wide commitment to lifelong learning and continual growth, which fueled innovation throughout the company. Creativity and innovation were evident, especially in on-the-spot adaptations to unfamiliar field settings or dynamic weather changes. The chief executive officer (CEO) mentored employees and others outside the company and freely shared his experience as a successful entrepreneur. Before taking calculated risks, company leaders engaged leaders and employees in an examination of literature from leading authors. Leaders also conducted a critical review of pertinent data and encouraged spirited internal dialogue through which participants created new strategies and tactics that helped maintain the competitive edge.

Critical Finding: Commitment to Lifelong Learning Stimulates Innovation and Growth

Bennet and Bennet (2003) noted companies "at the forefront of organizational performance [are] knowledge-based organizations [that adopt best practices and are] employee-centered, team-based, networked...and knowledge intense structures" (p. 14). The summer of 2009 was an especially dynamic and uncertain time when many clients held off planning large corporate events because of the economic downturn. Without ample time to forecast and plan the typically heavy summer picnic season, company leaders faced the daunting challenge of executing rapid, accelerated responses to last-minute decisions to proceed with events. Operating close to the 'edge of chaos' required an intelligent, complex adaptive system that integrated human and mechanical knowledge effectively (Bennet & Bennet, 2003; Thompson, 2007). Operating near the edge provided "opportunities for creativity and innovation" that relied on "the motivation and freedom of individual agents" (Bennet & Bennet, 2003, p. 16) to exploit and maximize efforts, and employees learned and gained from these challenges by being flexible and committed to change as situations required.

Impact of the Company on External Parties

Clients and customers. Character-based culture had a very positive impact upon clients and customers because of the relationships that developed between employees and those they served. Despite cost-cutting measures clients used to deal with a tighter economy, most clients used the caterer's ability to provide a unique and memorable experience along with ease of service as critical determinants rather than price when selecting a caterer. Receiving exceptional service and knowing their customers would not be disappointed drove clients to seek the quality provider when the client's reputation was on the line. To ensure the company provided consistent excellent service, company leaders sought the right people who would exemplify company core values.

Suppliers. Suppliers also preferred working with leaders and employees who showed zeal and passion for their work and business. Leaders worked to align their character-based culture with suppliers who were equally committed to excellence and had the best quality products. Leaders developed long-term, trust-based relationships with their best suppliers rather than arms-length transactions common to many businesses. The durability and strength of these relationships stemmed from conscious alignment with shared values.

Advisory board. Relationships with members of the advisory board reflected a similar alignment of core values. Board members provided a multi-disciplinary cross-sectional view of best industry practices, and some board members served as internal consultants and functional experts who shared their experiences from a wide range of industries. Leaders and employees viewed board members as partners in expanding organizational knowledge.

THE RIVER OF CHARACTER

Kow (2004) noted, "In the world of business, the only thing that really matters is organizational performance" (p. 281). The study showed how organizational performance depends upon human factors, especially within the relationships through which people achieve individual and organizational objectives. The study emphasized the interdependence of individual performances related to specific organizational functions required to satisfy customer needs. The study revealed how an invisible River of Character flows through an organization; the following paragraphs briefly describe the foundations of this river.

Wheatley (1992) noted that if organizations were machines, then attempts to control them would make sense, but "if organizations are process structures, then seeking to impose control through permanent structure is suicide" (p. 23). Organizations are indeed process structures comprised of unique human beings with unique needs. Organizations are "patterns of communications and relations among a group of human beings, including the processes for making and implementing decisions" (Simon, 1997. p. 18). Understanding organizations as patterns of communications and relations helps define character-based culture, which relies on three additional concepts: flow, transcendence, and positive deviance.

Flow

The human brain processes thousands of automatic operations every minute, and each process includes a series of complex mental operations that occur in fractions of a second (Csikszentmihalyi, 1990). According to Csikszentmihalyi (1990), each process retrieves "appropriate references from memory [while evaluating an event and selecting the] right thing to do" (p. 31) from stored memory with lightning-fast timing; this memory retrieval relies on attention, which is a form of *psychic energy* necessary for getting work done. Without attention, "no work can be done, and in doing work [attention] is dissipated" (Csikszentmihalyi, p. 33).

How one invests psychic energy determines how thoughts, feelings, and memories will be shaped and used (Csikszentmihalyi, 1990). Psychic disorder, or psychic entropy, adversely affects this consciousness and attention by feeding information to the brain that either "conflicts with existing intentions" (Csikszentmihalyi, p. 36) or distracts one from carrying out intentions. The optimal experience, where information that flows into consciousness is "congruent with goals," (Csikszentmihalyi, p. 39) opposes psychic entropy and results in *flow*, a key concept within the culture of character .

Transcendence

According to Pratt and Ashforth (2003), "Individuals actively desire and seek meaningfulness in their lives and work" (p. 310). Meaningfulness exists *in* work and *at* work. Meaningfulness *in* work centers primarily on the person through employee involvement and job redesign practices. Meaningfulness *at* work describes "organizations that focus only on enriching one's organizational membership" rather than on the work itself (Pratt & Ashforth, p. 317).

Yet, meaningfulness exists in another form. Transcendence includes the loosely coupled phenomena of connecting to "something greater than oneself" and integrating one's identity and traits "into a roughly coherent system" (Pratt & Ashforth, 2003, p. 322) that helps one achieve aspirations and potential. Transcendence involves a "comprehensive system of beliefs" (Pratt & Ashforth, p. 323) that connects and explains one's identity, values and purpose, and ideology, a system that cultures of character closely resemble.

Positive Deviance

Psychologists "define deviance as intentional behavior that significantly departs from norms" (Spreitzer & Sonenshein, 2003, p. 208). Although most literature views deviance in negative terms, "departures from norms can also be positive or constructive" (Spreitzer & Sonenshein, p. 209). Virtuous behaviors are positive deviations from the norms of society (Spreitzer & Sonenshein). Positive deviance reflects the two dimensions of character, where performance character concerns doing the *best* job one can do and moral character reflects being the *best* person one can be toward others (Lickona & Davidson, 2005). Performance and moral character represent honorable or virtuous behaviors; thus, to exercise character means showing positive deviance related to societal norms.

The River of Character Within Company Culture

Organizational culture is messy, complex, and complicated because people are involved. Dealing with culture requires a broader, systemic view of the business and the universe within which the business operates. Some business owners struggle because they fail to embrace the importance of culture for sustainable business success and lack an appreciation of the systems for which they are responsible. Deming (1994) defined a system of profound knowledge that placed an appreciation of the system of business at the pinnacle of any business model. If a leader at the top does not understand the system that comprises the business, he or she can expect much less of the employees upon whom organizational performance depends.

Within the system of profound knowledge, Deming (1994) noted three other critical elements of a business: (a) the theories that support the business, (b) the concept and understanding of variation, and (c) a strong understanding of psychology. Deming considered psychology critical because human nature and the variability of human behavior add to organizational complexity. By aligning personal values with organizational values, organizational leaders reduce variation within the organization and gain close alignment between the efforts of employees and the objectives to which employees direct their efforts. Thus, understanding variation in human behavior requires an understanding of character.

Character-based cultures have the potential for changing the communities and societies in which they operate. McCullough and Snyder (2000) suggested that the definition of *virtue* should expand to "psychological processes that consistently enables [*sic*] a person to think and act so as to yield benefits for him-or herself [*sic*] *and* society" (p. 3). This definition presents a systemic view of the impact of virtue upon external parties, not merely those with whom one has immediate contact. Taking a systemic view of virtues suggests that the virtues of individuals intersect, complement, and strengthen the virtues of others through which others outside the immediate circle of influence can feel ripple effects.

Leaders must take a systemic view of business and engage all members of their organizations in creating and nurturing character-based culture (Turknett & Turknett, 2005). According to Turknett and Turknett (2005), "Creating a culture of character . . . requires that each of us believe that part of our purpose on this earth is to become better people" (p. 4). Within any business enterprise, taking "individual responsibility for every family, team, community, or organization" to which one belongs means taking responsibility for the ethics and daily conduct through which a business achieves success, growth, and profit (Turknett & Turknett, p. 4). This responsibility resides with the River of Character that exists within any organization.

Building Organizational Energy and Effectiveness Through the River of Character

Figure 2 represents a model of character-based culture in the form of a flowing river. The river begins with the performance and moral character traits and practices within each employee. The lower left side of the model represents key performance character traits employees bring to the company while the right lower side of the model represents the moral character traits employees also bring

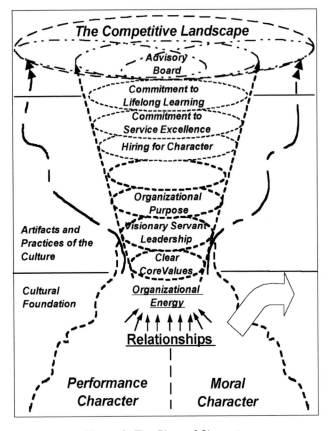

Figure 2: The River of Character

(Lickona & Davidson, 2005). Using the left and right sides of the brain within the model is purposeful. The left-brain side represents the intrapersonal competences of emotional intelligence, such as self-awareness while the right-brain side represents the interpersonal competences of emotional intelligence, such as relational competence (Cherniss & Goleman, 2001).

The study identified specific left-brain, performance character traits, such as knowledge of the business, personal courage, professionalism, and personal accountability for actions and outcomes that were necessary for employees to do their best job. Individual traits that reflected right-brain moral character and the desire to be the best person one could be toward others consisted of some grounding in Judeo-Christian principles coupled with the moral beliefs of the founders or moral teachings to which employees were exposed during the course of their personal development. Moral character traits arose from these foundations and included views about fairness, citizenship, and teamwork as well as an orientation to serving others.

The more closely one identifies with organizational traits such as values, the faster and easier assimilation into company life becomes. When assimilation fails to occur, individual psychic energy is incompatible with the prevailing culture, and an escape valve must exist. Much like a dam with an overflow spillway, an exit path must exist for those who do not fit the culture. Individuals whose psychic energy is out of synchronization with others in the organization should leave the organization.

Employees in character-based cultures become immersed in the company because they closely identify with the organizational belief system and values of others with whom they relate on a daily basis. The foundations of lasting relationships are trust and care (Nonaka & Nishiguchi, 2001). The flow within relationships and the values embedded in the relationships anneal with company values, which convert individual energies within the river into organizational energy.

Annealing Values and Directing Organizational Energy

The artifacts and practices of the character-based culture serve to integrate and anneal individual character traits for organizational effectiveness. Without a coordinating and central focus, individual efforts easily dissipate with little effect. Leaders have primary responsibility for embedding culture through the things to which they pay attention, measure, and control (Schein, 2004). Having a simplified core of internal influence allows leaders to pay attention to, measure, and control major areas of the culture while allowing managers and employees to pay attention to smaller items.

Individual characters begin to anneal with traits of others through relationships that feed organizational energy, which drives performance and results within the organization. Organizational energy and the focus of individual attention closely relate to mindfulness found in high reliability organizations (Weick & Sutcliffe, 2001). Mindful people are highly attentive because they constantly anticipate the next potential failure and the actions necessary to neutralize or eliminate problems to avoid failure (Weick & Sutcliffe). Thus, the positive deviance of character directly affects sustainability of operations because people think and look ahead and act accordingly to satisfy customers, avoid problems, and overcome obstacles.

Creating Value for Clients and Customers

Organizational energy flows through the four artifacts and three core practices in the order shown in Figure 2. Clients, customers, and suppliers are the primary evaluators of organizational effectiveness. The organizational energy that flows within the River of Character depends upon the purity of trust and caring within relationships throughout the organization.

Dysfunctional behaviors pollute relationships as toxins and trash interfere with healthy rivers. Virtuous relationships within a character-based company reflect positive psychic energy rather than the negative deviance evident in dysfunctional behaviors within other organizations. Thus, to ensure a healthy organization void of dysfunctional behaviors and to achieve optimal organizational performance and effectiveness, organizational leaders first need to model performance and moral character throughout their organizations. Leaders must also hire people of strong character and nurture a culture of character to keep the underlying River of Character running as clean as possible through their organization.

CONCLUSION

Leaders must accept and fulfill their responsibility to lead rather than simply manage. Leaders must engage their right brains more fully, especially the areas that deal with moral character and higher levels of emotional intelligence. Just as leadership models exist to guide, the River of Character exists to guide leaders in creating character-based culture.

The ethnographic research study that discovered the River of Character explored the impact of a character-based culture on the internal coherence of business practices. The literature implied that leaders in the 21st century must be people of strong character with exceptional cultural and emotional intelligence to face a myriad of challenges in the workplace. The study showed how the alignment of artifacts and practices of character-based culture direct the River of Character to achieve high organizational energy. Organizational energy translates into positive internal effects on employees, leaders, and advisers, exceptional outcomes for clients and customers, and effectiveness for the organization through customer loyalty, positive buying decisions, profitability, and corporate sustainability. The

River of Character shows how leaders can build character-based culture to create organizational energy, increase organizational effectiveness, and achieve sustainable, profitable performance.

References

Albrecht, K. (1988). *At America's service*. New York, NY: Warner Books, Inc.

Angrosino, M. (2007). *Doing ethnographic and observational research* (1st ed.). Thousand Oaks, CA: SAGE Publications, Inc.

Argandoña, A. (2003). Fostering values in organizations. *Journal of Business Ethics, 45*(1/2, Part 2), 15–28.

Arjoon, S. (2000). Virtue theory as a dynamic theory of business. *Journal of Business Ethics, 28*(2), 159–178.

Badaracco, J. L. (1998, March-April). The discipline of character. *Harvard Business Review, 76*(2), 114–124

Beinhocker, E., Davis, I., & Mendonca, L. (2009, July-August). The 10 trends you have to watch. *Harvard Business Review, 87*(7/8), 55–60.

Benedetto, R. (2009). *An ethnographic study of character-based culture in a small business setting* (Unpublished doctoral dissertation). University of Phoenix, Phoenix, AZ.

Bennet, D., & Bennet, A. (2003). The rise of the knowledge organization. In C. Holsapple (Ed.) *Handbook on knowledge management 1: Knowledge matters* (1st ed.): 5–20. New York, NY: Springer-Verlag.

Birnholtz, J. P., Cohen, M. D., & Hoch, S. V. (2007, March-April). Organizational character: On the regeneration of Camp Poplar Grove. *Organization Science, 18*(2), 315–332.

Bowen, S. A. (2004, July). Organizational factors encouraging ethical decision making: An exploration into the case of an exemplar. *Journal of Business Ethics, 52*(4), 311–324.

Bragues, G. (2008). The ancients against the moderns: Focusing on the character of corporate leaders. *Journal of Business Ethics, 78*(3), 373–387.

Brien, A. (1998). Professional ethics and the culture of trust. *Journal of Business Ethics, 17*(4), 391–409.

Brown, M. E., Treviño, L. K., & Harrison, D. A. (2005). Ethical leadership: A social learning perspective for construct development and testing. *Organizational Behavior and Human Decision Processes, 97*(2), 117–134.

Bruhn, J. G. (2005). Looking good, but behaving badly: Leader accountability and ethics failure. *The Health Care Manager, 24*(3), 191–199.

Burns, J. M. (1978). *Leadership.* New York, NY: Harper & Row.

Cameron, K. (2003). Organizational virtuousness and performance. In. K. S. Cameron, J. E.Dutton, & R. E. Quinn (Eds.). *Positive organizational scholarship: Foundations of a new discipline* (pp. 48–65). San Francisco, CA: Berrett-Koehler Publishers, Inc.

Cameron, K. (2006). Good or not bad: Standards and ethics in managing change. *Academy of Management Learning & Education, 5*(3), 317–323.

Carroll, A. B. (2000). Ethical challenges for business in the new millennium: Corporate social responsibility and models of management morality. *Business Ethics Quarterly, 10*(1), 33–42.

Carter, S. L. (1998). *Civility: Manners, morals, and the etiquette of democracy.* New York, NY: Basic Books.

Cherniss, C., & Goleman, D. (Eds.). (2001). *The emotionally intelligent workplace.* San Francisco, CA: Jossey-Bass.

Chowdhury, S. (2003). Toward the future of organization. In. S. Chowdhury (Ed.). *Organization 21C:* 1–18. Upper Saddle River, NJ: Financial Times Prentice Hall.

Chun, R. (2005). Ethical character and virtue of organizations: An empirical assessment and strategic implications. *Journal of Business Ethics, 57*(3), 269–284.

Collins, J. (2001). *Good to great.* New York, NY: Harper Collins Publishers, Inc.

Collins, J., & Porras, J. (1994). *Built to last.* New York, NY: HarperBusiness.

Coulon, A. (1995). *Ethnomethodology.* Thousand Oaks, CA: SAGE Publications, Inc.

Csikszentmihalyi, M. (1990). *Flow.* New York, NY: Harper Collins.

Deming, W. E. (1994). *The new economics for industry, government and education* (2nd ed.). Cambridge, MA: The Massachusetts Institute of Technology.

Dickson, M. W., Smith, D. B., Grojean, M. W., & Ehrhart, M. (2001). An organizational climate regarding ethics: The outcome of leader values and the practices that reflect them. *The Leadership Quarterly, 12*(2), 197–217.

Goleman, D. (1995). *Emotional intelligence.* New York, NY: Bantam Books.

Goleman, D. (2000, March-April). Leadership that gets results. *Harvard Business Review, 78*(2), 78–90.

Greenleaf, R. K. (1977). *Servant leadership.* New York, NY: Paulist Press.

Grojean, M. W., Resick, C. J., Dickson, M. W., & Smith, D. B. (2004). Leaders, values, and organizational climate: Examining leadership strategies for establishing an organizational climate regarding ethics. *Journal of Business Ethics, 55*(3), 223–241.

Hamel, G. (2009, February). Moon shots for management. *Harvard Business Review, 87*(2), 91–98.

Hartman, E. M. (2006). Can we teach character? An Aristotelian answer. *Academy of Management Learning & Education, 5*(1), 68–81.

Heenan, D., & Bennis, W. (1999). *Co-leaders.* New York, NY: John Wiley & Sons, Inc.

Hitt, W. D. (1990). *Ethics and leadership.* Columbus, OH: Batelle Press.

Hofstede, G., & Hofstede, G. J. (2005). *Cultures and organizations.* New York, NY: McGraw-Hill.

Kotter, J. P. (1996). *Leading change.* Boston, MA: Harvard Business School Press.

Kow, G. (2004, December). Turning around business performance: Part II. *Journal of Change Management, 4*(4), 281–296.

Latham, J., & Vinyard, J. (2005). *Baldrige user's guide.* New York, NY: Wiley.

Lickona, T., & Davidson, M. (2005). *Smart and good high schools* (1st ed.). Cortland, NY: Center for the 4th and 5th Rs (Respect & Responsibility).

Margulies, N., & Raia, A. (1994). The significance of core values on the theory and practice of organizational development. *Journal of Organizational Change Management, 1*(1), 6–17.

McCabe, D. L., Trevino, L. K., & Butterfield, K. D. (1996). The influence of collegiate and corporate codes of conduct on ethics-related behavior in the workplace. *Business Ethics Quarterly, 6*(4), 461–476.

McCullough, M. E., & Snyder, C. R. (2000, Spring). Classical sources of human strength: Revisiting an old home and building a new one. *Journal of Social and Clinical Psychology, 19*(1), 1–10.

McFarland, K. R. (2008). *The breakthrough company.* New York, NY: Crown Business.

McMahon, T. F. (1991). A reaction to Vogel's "The ethical roots of business." *Business Ethics Quarterly, 1*(2), 211–222.

Meglino, B. M., & Ravlin, E. C. (1998). Individual values in organizations: Concepts, controversies, and research. *Journal of Management, 24*(3), 351–389.

Mitroff, I. I. (2004). *Crisis leadership.* Hoboken, NJ: John Wiley and Sons, Inc.

Neilson, G., Pasternack, B. A., & Mendes, D. (2004, Summer). The 7 types of organizational DNA. *Strategy+business,* (35), 95–103.

Nonaka, I., & Nishiguchi, T. (Eds.). (2001). *Knowledge emergence.* New York, NY: Oxford University Press.

O'Toole, J., & Bennis, W. (2009, June). What's needed next: A culture of candor. *Harvard Business Review, 87*(6), 54–61.

Pratt, M. G., & Ashforth, B. E. (2003). Fostering meaningfulness in working and at work. In S. Srivastva & D. Cooperrider *Appreciative management and leadership* (Rev. ed.): 309–327. Euclid, OH: Williams Custom Publishing.

Schein, E. H. (2004). *Organizational culture and leadership* (3rd ed.). San Francisco, CA: Jossey-Bass.

Scott, E. D. (2002). Organizational moral values. *Business Ethics Quarterly, 12*(1), 33–55.

Simon, H. A. (1997). *Administrative behavior* (4th ed.). New York, NY: The Free Press.

Sims, R. R., & Brinkmann, J. (2002). Leaders as moral role models: The case of John Gutfreund at Salomon Brothers. *Journal of Business Ethics, 35*(4), 327–339.

Spreitzer, G. M., & Sonenshein, S. (2003). Positive deviance and extraordinary organizing. In S. Srivastva & D. Cooperrider *Appreciative management and leadership* (Rev. ed.): 207–224. Euclid, OH: Williams Custom Publishing.

Tang, V., & Bauer, R. (1995). *Competitive dominance.* New York, NY: Van Nostrand Reinhold.

Thompson, J. D. (2007). *Organizations in action.* New Brunswick, NJ: Transaction Publishers.

Treacy, M., & Wiersema, F. (1993, January-February). Customer intimacy and other value disciplines. *Harvard Business Review, 71*(1), 84–93.

Treacy, M., & Wiersema, F. (1995). *The discipline of market leaders.* Reading, MA: Addison-Wesley Publishing Company, Inc.

Turknett, R. L., & Turknett, C. N. (2005). *Decent people, decent company.* Mountain View, CA: Davies-Black Publishing.

Van Lee, R., Fabish, L., & McGaw, N. (2005, Summer). The value of corporate values. *Strategy+business,* (39), 52–65.

Weick, K. E., & Sutcliffe, K. M. (2001). *Managing the unexpected.* San Francisco, CA: Jossey-Bass.

Wheatley, M. J. (1992). *Leadership and the new science.* San Francisco, CA: Berrett-Koehler Publishers, Inc.

About the Author

Dr. Ramon L. (Ray) Benedetto has a varied practitioner and academic background. Dr. Ray holds several nationally accredited degrees: a Bachelor of Science (BS) in Health Planning and Administration from Penn State; a Master of Science (MS) in Systems Management from the University of Southern California; and a Doctorate of Management (DM) in Organizational Leadership from the University of Phoenix School of Advanced Studies.

Dr. Ray, as he is known to his MBA students, teaches leadership and ethics for the University of Phoenix Chicago Campus. A Distinguished Military Graduate of the Air Force ROTC program at Penn State, Dr. Ray served on active duty for nearly 25 years, rising to the rank of Colonel before returning to civilian life. Dr. Ray has been heavily engaged in organizational transformation efforts in the public and private sectors for the past 30 years and leads a consulting firm that specializes in helping leaders in business, government, and community-based organizations build high-performing character-based cultures.

Dr. Ray is board certified in healthcare management and a Fellow of the American College of Healthcare Executives where he serves as a mentor. He is also an active member of the Academy of Management (AOM) where he serves as an academic reviewer and program contributor. He is currently working on a book about character-based business with leaders of several companies.

To reach Dr. Ray for information, please e-mail: ray@guidestar inc.com.

CHAPTER 7

The Impact That Ethics and Values Have On Leader-Follower Relationships

Dr. Susan K. Fan

In the 21st century, many companies are challenged with ethical dilemmas. Many leaders are questioned for their ethical behavior both professionally and personally. Is leadership ethics simply a matter of right or wrong? Or is it a matter of the leader's values and belief system? What is the relationship between values and ethics? What challenges do values and ethics have on leader-follower relationship? For example, a manager calls an employee, who was at home recuperating from major surgeries, that if he doesn't return to work within 2 weeks, he would be laid off. At that time, the recuperating employee was on medical leave of absence (MLOA) and planning to return to work within one month even though the original MLOA doesn't expire for another two months. Would this manager's actions be considered right or wrong? How would the manager's action impact their leader-follower relationship? For a second example, a hiring manager was interviewing candidates for a position. The hiring manager's boss told the hiring manager that he had to hire one particular interviewee regardless of qualification. If the hiring manager did what his boss asked him to do, would his actions be ethical or unethical, right or wrong? How would the manager's action impact the leader-follower relationship?

According to Bass and Steidlmeier (2004)

The ethics of leadership rests upon three pillars: (a) the moral character of the leader; (b) the ethical legitimacy of the values embedded in the leader's vision, articulation, and program which followers either embrace or reject; and (c) the morality of the processes of social ethical choice and action that leaders and followers engage in and collectively pursue. Such ethical characteristics of leadership have been widely acknowledged (Wren, 1998; Kouzes & Posner, 1993; Greenleaf, 1977; Conger & Kanungo, 1998). (as cited in Ciulla, 2004, pp. 175–176)

Since leadership ethics is a very broad topic, the discussion in this chapter will focus on what influence ethics and values have on leader-follower relationship with respect to the findings from the Fan 2006 study.

The Fan study, conducted in 2006, investigated the research question: How do the congruent values between leaders and members relate to team performance? (Fan, 2006) The following Hypotheses were posed to answer the research question:

$H1_0$: There is no relationship between the congruent values of leaders and of members on team performance.

$H1$: There is a relationship between congruent values of leaders and of members on team performance.

The Belief Systems Audit by Williams (2000) was employed to study the congruency of values between the leaders and their respective team members. The research methodology included both quantitative and qualitative data collection. Six different analysis techniques were applied to determine the relationship between congruent values between leaders and team members with team performance (Fan, 2006).

THEORETICAL FRAMEWORK

Values are believed to be the motivational force behind a person's dreams, behaviors, and actions (Rokeach, 1979; Stackman, Pinder, & Connor, 2000). Values can also reflect that which is deemed important, a priority, or precious in a person's mind (Baron & Spranca, 1997). Values are often used to describe what is important to organizations, that is, cultural values or organization values. Furthermore, values are predictive of the leadership style of a person and the kind of approach each team member might take toward completing a task (Zaccaro, Rittman & Marks, 2001). If values define how much something is worth or the degree of importance something is to an individual or an organization, then ethics can be considered as the code of conduct. If one acts or behaves against the code of conduct, it would be considered as unethical. For example, there is the familiar Enron case where top-level management team members behaved unethically. In this case, there was a big gap between the set of values the company set and the resulting CEOs' actions. Rost asserted:

> Leadership is an influence relationship wherein leaders and followers propose real changes that reflect their mutual purposes. . . the ethics of the leadership process requires that the leaders and followers use influence in their interactions to achieve this mutuality. All other behaviors are unethical in a leadership relationship. (1991, p.161)

Both ethics and values can influence a person's behavior, action, or conduct,

Kouzes and Posner (1993) noted that the credibility of leadership depended on its moral purpose, trust, and the hopes it engendered. Leaders are seen as obligated and responsible for the moral environment of their group, organization, or society (Greenleaf 1977). A major task for leaders is bringing together their followers around common values (Fairholm 1991). The leaders themselves, often are seen as the embodiment of such values (McCollough 1991). And just as when leaders are more competent, those they lead are more effective, so when leaders are more morally mature, those they lead display higher moral reasoning (Dukerich, Nichols, et al. 1990). (as cited in Ciulla 1998–2004. p. 170)

Williams (1993) posited that if the values of a leader and the follower are congruent, effective team performance would be the side effect. Having congruence in values does not mean that each person views the world the same way, but rather there would be "congruence of each person and each system that allows the system to operate effectively" (Williams, 2000, p. 2).

FAN STUDY FINDINGS AND ANALYSES

The findings showed that half of the leaders who participated in the Fan study held the highest scores in psychological factors of the Values Survey. This means these leaders felt that "people are essential and you work hard at aligning yourself with others who challenge and accept challenges" (Williams, 1993, p. 183). This also suggests that their belief system enables them to appreciate each individual team member as well as the team and they will proactively rather than reactively face issues (Williams, p. 184). According to Williams (1993), the scores from the values survey are divided into three belief systems categories: theological, legal, and psychological. Individuals whose highest score is in the theological category have a preference toward structure and rules, dislike changes, and feel better when they belong to a select group of people. If the highest score falls in the legal category, a person shows a tendency to be flexible and an ability to change based on attaining more control, authority, or power. This person also has a preference for structure and rules; however, the main desire is to maintain organizational stability. If the highest scores fall in the psychological category, that person has a need for change and to be in control of events that have a personal impact. There is also a strong need to feel involved with all aspects of change (Williams, 1993).

In order to explore the impact ethics and values have on leader-follower relationship, the author will reference findings from the research question posed in Fan study: How do the congruent values between leaders and members relate to team performance? (Fan, 2006) The Fan study indicated that successful leader-member relationships tend to share similar values of integrity, trustworthiness, the ability to listen to others, respect for others, courage, persistence, and exemplarity (Fan, 2006). Two kinds of quantitative data analysis were performed to determine the relationship between congruent values and team performance. One involved statistical testing and the other consisted of pattern recognition using graphical illustrations of data. Both methods provided a means for data analysis that led to the findings and results. Lastly, qualitative data was collected from interviews with randomly selected participants for triangulation purposes.

Quantitative Data

With the sample population of 14 leaders and 103 team members, the independent variable, congruent values, was measured with the leader's scores and the team member's scores. Six different analysis techniques were applied to determine the relationship between congruent values between leaders and team members with team performance. First, the researcher derived mean scores of the values of the leaders and the team members. The values were found to be significantly different. The leaders group rated high in the theological category whereas the members group rated high in the legal category. According to Williams (1993), this result means that the leaders prefer structure and rules, dislikes changes, and prefers to work with a select group of familiar people. Members of the teams tend to be flexible and possess an ability to change based on attaining either more control, authority, or power. Team members also prefer structure and rules, although their main desire is to maintain organizational stability (Williams).

Second, the analysis came from computing the Pearson's correlation coefficient (p value) using the mean average scores from leaders and members. The results showed a mild but insignificant correlation between the leaders group and the members group at the psychological level but there was no discernible relationship at the theological level. All the p values were higher than the conventional 0.05 level of significance. Third, the analysis involved using correlation analysis for each values category (i.e., theological, legal, and psychological) by pairing each member's scores with his or her leader's score. The results (See Tables 1, 2, and 3 on the following pages) provided another perspective of the relationship between the leaders and their respective team members. It was revealed that within the same team, the leader and his or her team members showed a slight relationship with regard to legal congruence ($p = 0.06$) but no significant relationship with regard to the theological and psychological values' congruence with each other. This does not take into consideration the relationship to team performance.

Fourth, the analysis involved the use of graphic illustration to investigate the relationship between each team leader with his or her team members and team performance. For each performance rating of exceeds, meets, or below expectations, respectively, two teams were selected for a graphic evaluation. To understand whether there

TABLE 1. CORRELATION BETWEEN TEAM LEADER AND MEMBERS ON A THEOLOGICAL LEVEL

	Team member's theological score	His or her leader's theological score
TEAM MEMBER'S THEOLOGICAL SCORE		
Pearson correlation	1	−.16
Sig. (2-tailed)		.13
N	103	103
HIS OR HER LEADER'S THEOLOGICAL SCORE		
Pearson correlation	−.16	1
Sig. (2-tailed)	.12	
N	103	103

TABLE 2. CORRELATION BETWEEN TEAM LEADER AND MEMBERS ON LEGAL LEVEL

	Team member's legal score	His or her leader's legal score
TEAM MEMBER'S LEGAL SCORE		
Pearson correlation	1	.19
Sig. (2-tailed)		.06
N	103	103
HIS OR HER LEADER'S LEGAL SCORE		
Pearson correlation	.19	1
Sig. (2-tailed)	.06	
N	103	103

TABLE 3. CORRELATION BETWEEN TEAM LEADER AND MEMBERS ON PSYCHOLOGICAL LEVEL

	Team member's psychological score	His or her leader's psychological score
TEAM MEMBER'S PSYCHOLOGICAL SCORE		
Pearson correlation	1	.16
Sig. (2-tailed)		.12
N	103	103
HIS OR HER LEADER'S PSYCHOLOGICAL SCORE		
Pearson correlation	.16	1
Sig. (2-tailed)	.12	
N	103	103

was congruence in the values scores between each team leader and his or her team members, the researcher looked for patterns in the figures and check for any apparent correlations between congruence of values and team performance. For example, the graphic illustration (see Figure 1) demonstrated no relation between team performance and the congruent values between a leader and his or her team members.

The above techniques did not reveal any significant findings of the relationship between congruent values and team performance, the researcher chose to examine in depth the relationship between each leader and his or her team members for each of the three value categories using ANOVA to determine if any correlation existed between the teams and within the teams and if there are statistically significant differences among the teams or factors. The data used for performing ANOVA derived from the average sum squares of the

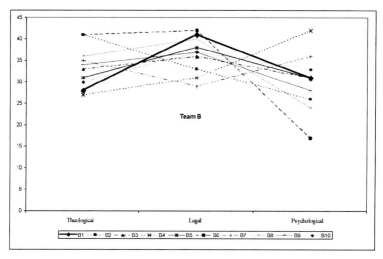

Figure 1. Team B exceeded performance goals.

difference between leader and member scores. From the two ANOVA tables, the average for each group and the variances are very close together while the variances were relatively large. If the *F* value is greater than the *F*-critical value, then the hypothesis that the three values categories differ can be rejected. In this case, the 0.05 level of significance with two degrees of freedom was used. The hypothesis that the three value categories differ could not be rejected based on the average sum squares of the difference between leader and member scores. Thus there were no significant differences within the groups or between the groups.

The last analysis focused on the values scores of the leaders' group and team performance for four quarters and the values scores of the members group and team performance for the same four quarters of the year. Tables 4 and 5 showed *p* values from the *F* test; leaders' theological scores were significantly associated with team performance ratings in Q1 and Q2. The team members' psychological scores were found significantly related to the team performance rating for Quarters 1, 2, and 4.

The F-test is a test of the null hypothesis that group means on the dependent variable do not differ. It is used to test the significance of each main and interaction effect. A "p" probability value of .05 or less on the F test conventionally leads the researcher to conclude the effect is real and not due to chance of sampling. ("Univariate GLM, ANOVA, and ANCOVA," n.d., p. 12)

TABLE 4. CORRELATION BETWEEN VALUES OF LEADERS AND TEAM PERFORMANCE

	Q1	Q2	Q3	Q4
Theological	0.04	0.04	0.42	0.54
Legal	0.45	0.45	0.99	0.87
Psychological	0.94	0.94	0.23	0.28

TABLE 5. CORRELATION BETWEEN VALUES OF MEMBERS AND TEAM PERFORMANCE

	Q1	Q2	Q3	Q4
Theological	0.33	0.33	0.99	0.97
Legal	0.17	0.17	0.45	0.23
Psychological	0.04	0.04	0.42	0.05

Finally, in response to the research question in the Fan Study that asked, how do the congruent values between leaders and members relate to team performance, the answer was that there is no evidence of congruent values between leaders and members with team performance within each team or between the leaders group and the members group. There is significance in the correlation between leaders and team performance and members and team performance in different categories of values (i.e., theological, legal, and psychological). The null hypothesis relating to this research question: There is no relationship between the congruent values of leaders and of members on team performance, could not be rejected (Fan, 2006).

Qualitative Findings

Respect for followers was the highest average rated characteristics for both personal importance and for respondents' leaders. Listening, courage, and being an example was rated the second highest importance for respondents and listening was rated second highest on how participant leaders were rated. Integrity and trust were rated the third most important to respondents and persistence and courage were the highest among the leader's rating (see Figure 2).

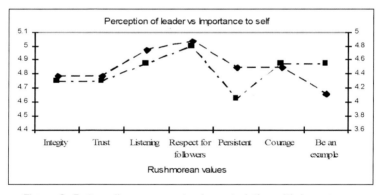

Figure 2. Bottom line represents characteristics with importance to participants and top line represents characteristics perceived in their leaders.

The eight interview participants consisted of five leaders and three team members, four female and four male, all answered the same questions posed by the researcher (see Appendix A). The researcher purposefully developed eight questions for the interview participants that were different than those questions found in the surveys in order to gain an extra perspective on the participants regarding congruent values and leadership style with team performance. Questions 1 and 2 served as warm-up questions and confirmed demographics gathered in Part 1 of the surveys. Questions 3 and 4 aimed at leadership style while Questions 7 and 8 aimed at values. Questions 5 and 6 were used to confirm performance rating. In essence, in this triangulation process, the researcher wanted to investigate if among the interview participants, regardless of their position, there was any correlation between their perception of their leader's leadership characteristics and their personal rating of the importance of these leadership characteristics.

The data in Figure 2 indicate that the four closest related traits— integrity, trust, respect for followers and courage—were very important to the interview participants and the same characteristics were perceived in their leaders. The seven values listed in the figure are those described by O'Toole (1996) as the Rushmorean values. O'Toole believed that these seven values are essential for good leadership. In Question 7, the participants were asked to rate the degree to which they believe their leader possesses each of these seven Rushmorean values. For Question 8, the participants were asked to rate the degree of importance of these 7 values to themselves. The scale for Questions 7 and 8 was from 1 (lowest) to 5 (highest).

During the interview, each participant was asked to describe what successful leadership meant to them personally and summarize successful leadership in one sentence for the researcher (see Appendix A, Question 3). The participants' responses were as follows:

B-Manager: "A successful leader is someone that is a good listener, consistently opens to new ideas and wanting to challenge you to the next level. Helping my staff to be their best is my goal." (B-Manager's team rating was 'exceeds' for four quarters.)

B-Member: "A successful leader is someone that develops people under them rather than become their baby-sitter, delegate to team members and shows them the responsibility, knows the potential of the followers and brings out their competitive nature in a positive way, help everyone be their best. Be honest and have trust, accommodates but also be a mentor, passes the passion and skills of their job to their followers. When you do a good job, and then ask yourself what you did differently to achieve such results." (B-Member's team rating was 'exceeds' for four quarters and is staff of B-Manager.)

C-Member: "A successful leader is someone who respects and listens to you. Being a motivator and takes staff to the next level. Not just a title but needs to demonstrate the leader's ability to staff. Someone whose followers can believe in." (C-Member is from a team with performance rating 'exceeds.')

E-Member: "A successful leader is someone that leads by example and has the ability to motivate. Efficient." (E-Member is from a team whose performance rating was 'meets.')

F-Manager: "A successful leader is someone that does beyond their job." (F-Manager is from a team with performance rating "exceeds" for two quarter and then 'below' for two quarters.)

G-Manager: "A successful leader is someone that leads by example, even though it's hard, work the fun way and have a sense of humor. Set a good example in the beginning and balance all the good things. Need to have passion to work here." (G-Manager is from a team with performance rating 'exceeds.')

J-Manager: "A successful leader is someone that helps their staff meet goals, to coach team members to full potential so they are also success - ful." (J-Manager is from a team that has performance rating 'below.')

K-Manager: "A successful leader is someone that is a role model about activity and process, need to be an expert to coach. Need to show the ability to the staff and earn their trust. Ask questions about tasks to help them along to a better place, get them to see it rather than just tell them." (K-Manager is from a team with performance rating 'meets.')

When asked to use single words to describe a good leader, the interview participants' response was as follows. The eight participants listed 33 different words in this exercise and three words were named repeatedly: *successful, honesty,* and *communications.* Table 6 lists all the words named.

TABLE 6. WORDS FROM PARTICIPANTS DESCRIBING A GOOD LEADER

Communications	Credible	Dedication
Team playing	Approachable	Fair
Good listener	Engaged	Successful
Honesty	Enthusiastic	Energetic
Able to handle objections	Level-headed and not super-emotional	Mentor
Respectful	Present both mentally & physically	Relator
Friendly		Coach
Kind	Business-like	Positive
Negotiator	Excellence	Commitment
Resourceful	Balanced kind of pushy	Discipline
		Integrity

Additional Findings

There was no confirmation of either values that related to team performance from the data analysis, which was structured around the research question. Thus, the researcher chose to test for possible additional discoveries by testing values of leaders and members separately with demographics predictors. The results show the p value from the F test of simple regression models using each of the values' score as the dependent and each of the demographics variables as the independent. For values and demographics, in regards to the leaders, the p values suggested significant association between the values of the leaders with age, gender, and education, but not for theological and education. For the team members, there was significant association between individual values scores for age, gender, and education. There was no association between theological and gender or between psychological and gender.

In regard to the correlation between the demographics variables and the three values categories (i.e., theological, legal, and psychological), there was a significant association found between the leaders' age, gender, and education with legal and psychological values that translated into leaders wanting stability and empowerment for their teams but preferring not to have rigid rules and structures. The team members' views of legal values differed according to gender, but there was no discernible difference in values with regard to their age or education.

CONCLUSIONS

All interpretations of the findings in the Fan Study were based on the definitions supplied by Williams (1993) regarding the three values categories. With regard to the values variable, half of the leaders who participated held the highest scores in psychological factors. Their belief system enables these leaders to appreciate each individual team member as well as the team and they proactively rather than reactively face issues (Williams, p. 184). Even though the survey instruments for values in this study did not lead to rejecting the null hypothesis, the findings from the interview participants yielded somewhat different results. This led to the conclusion that there appears to be a strong agreement between leaders and followers with regard to the seven Rushmorean values. Because only eight participants were interviewed, the results cannot be used to generalize the findings for the entire sample, but it can be used to facilitate innovative ideas for improving team performance and assisting future research.

How do ethics and values influence leader-follower relationships? Kouzes and Posner asserted (2002), "There's an ethical dimension to leadership that neither leaders nor constituents should take lightly. This is why we began our discussion of leadership practices with a focus on finding your voice–your authentic self grounded in a set of values and ideals" (p.392). And what might be some challenges that leader-follower relationship encounter in regards to ethical leadership? Rost's claim supported the Fan Study:

> Leadership is an influence relationship wherein leaders and followers propose real changes that reflect their mutual purposes. Since leaders and followers use influence to agree upon proposals for change that reflect their mutual purposes, they use their autonomy and value in the leadership relationship and do not have to sacrifice their integrity to belong to that relationship. (1993, p.161)

However, if a leader uses the power and authority given in the leadership position to manipulate or to abuse the follower in order to satisfy self-interests, then the opportunity for unethical actions could be unlimited,

> "achieving teamwork demands a concern for maintaining responsibility, accountability, authenticity, and integrity in the leader-follower relationship. Indeed, the often mentioned 'crisis of leadership' usually reveals an absence of these elements" (Ciulla, 2004, p. 56).

In summary, leadership comes with authority and power appropriate for the position given. The benefits and responsibilities within these leadership positions can ignite ethical challenges that could impact the leader-follower relationship. Leaders often find themselves using the power and authority given to their position to benefit self-interests. At the same time, their followers would experience the negative effects from the leader-follower relationship resulting in mistrusts of the leader. Leaders must remember that they need to be accountable not only for their decisions, actions, but also to their followers. The leaders who are self-seeking may cause followers to feel used and unsupported. In some cases, leaders might fault their followers for their own failures, thus, pushing the followers to place their loyalty elsewhere (Ciulla, 2004). The author concludes that leaders who lead with the followers' interests in mind would be less likely to act unethically than those that put their own interest first. Furthermore, the leaders who want to cultivate the leader-follower relationships are those that are more likely to have effective teams than those who don't. Lastly, the leaders who have successful leader-follower relationships are those that share common values and work towards common goals with their followers. The continuous growth of organizations is about cultivating leaders and potential leaders to recognize the importance of building their relationship with their followers. Successful organization is built on successful leader-follower relationships (Fan, 2006).

References

Baron, J., & Spranca, M. (1997). Protected values. *Organizational Behavior and Human Decision Processes, 70,* 1–16.

Ciulla, J. B. (Ed.). (1998). *Ethics: The heart of leadership.* Westport, CT: Praeger Publishers.

Ciulla, J. B. (Ed.). (2004). *Ethics, The heart of leadership* (2nd ed.). Westport, CT: Praeger.

Fan, S. K. (2006). The impact of congruent values and leadership styles on team performance in a financial institution. *Dissertations Abstracts International, 54,* (01), 534B. (UMI No. 3232325).

Kouzes, J. M., & Posner, B. Z. (2002). *The leadership challenge* (3rd ed.). San Francisco: Jossey-Bass.

Rokeach, M. (1979). *Understanding human values.* New York: Free Press.

Rost, J. (1991). *Leadership for the twenty-first century.* New York: Praeger.

Stackman, R. W., Pinder, C. C., & Connor, P. E. (2000). Values lost: Redirecting research on values in the workplace. In N. M. Ashkanasy, C. P. M. Wilderom, & M. F. Peterson (Eds.), *Handbook of organizational culture and climate.* Thousand Oaks, CA: Sage.

Univariate GLM, ANOVA, and ANCOVA. (n.d.). Retrieved from http://www2.chass.ncsu.edu/garson/PA765/anova.htm

Williams, L. C. (1993). *The congruence of people and organizations.* Westport, CT: Quorum Books.

Williams, L. C. (2000). *The belief system audit.* Phoenix, AZ: Institute for Transformative Thought and Learning.

Zaccaro, S. J., Rittman, A. L., & Marks, M. A. (2001). Team leadership. *Leadership Quarterly, 12,* 451–483.

APPENDIX A: INTERVIEW QUESTIONS

1. How many employees at this branch? What is the reporting structure?

2. How long have you been managing this team?

3. Please define in your own words what "successful leadership" is to you personally? If you have to summary to one sentence, what would you say?

4. Use single words to describe characteristics of a "good" leader?

5. How do you measure your team performance? Is it compared with other branches at the higher level of management?

6. Can you share with me this branch's ratings for the past year? Or can you tell me if this branch **met, exceeded,** or **did not meet** expectations when it comes to team performance goal for the past 4 quarters or year?

7. Please rate these characteristics as you see them in **your leader,** (1) you do not see this characteristic at all in your leader, (2) you see this characteristic once in a while in your leader, (3) you are not sure if this characteristic exists in your leader, (4) you see this characteristic often in your leader, (5) you see this characteristic consistently in your leader:

Integrity	1	2	3	4	5
Trust	1	2	3	4	5
Listening	1	2	3	4	5
Respect for followers	1	2	3	4	5
Persistent	1	2	3	4	5
Courage	1	2	3	4	5
Be an example	1	2	3	4	5

8. Please rate the importance of these characteristics to you personally, (1) being the least important to you, (2) being a little bit important to you, (3) you do not really care, (4) being very important to you, and (5) most important to you.

Integrity	1	2	3	4	5
Trust	1	2	3	4	5
Listening	1	2	3	4	5
Respect for followers	1	2	3	4	5
Persistent	1	2	3	4	5
Courage	1	2	3	4	5
Be an example	1	2	3	4	5

About the Author

Dr. Susan K. Fan holds several nationally accredited degrees: a Bachelor of Science (BSBA) in Business Administration; and a Master of Business Administration (MBA) from the John Sperling School of Business from University of Phoenix; and a Doctorate of Management (DM) in Organizational Leadership from the University of Phoenix, School of Advanced Studies.

Dr. Susan K. Fan has been working as a management professional in various leadership positions for companies in the Silicon Valley for the past 20 years such as Lockheed, Amdahl, Applied Materials, Silicon Graphics, and Intel Corporation. A few examples of Dr. Fan's professional experience include software design engineering, operations management, project management, international distribution channels establishment for new product marketing in Europe, Asia, and U.S.

Dr. Fan is working as an adjunct faculty with Kaplan University and Walden University.

Published works include her dissertation: *The impact of congruent values and leadership styles on team performance in a financial institution,* July 2006. *The Refractive Thinker: Vol. III: Change Management,* Chapter 8: *Successful Change Management Begins with Effective Leader-Follower Relationships.*

To reach Dr. Susan K. Fan, please e-mail: DrFan@aol.com.

Exploring the Transactional and Transformational Leadership Characteristics of Social Networking Communications

Dr. Gail Ferreira

The ability to harness the power of social networking software for business and personal communications has "flattened the world" (Friedman, 2006, p. 8), allowing leaders to converse directly with the general population using real-time messages (Friedman, 2006; G. Solomon & Schrum, 2007). Leaders must demonstrate specific characteristics to correspond effectively in a mutual exchange with their followers in order to compete as a global leader in the 21st century (Friedman, 2006). A new breed of global leaders, known as "Generation F leaders" (Hamel, 2009, ¶ 1), are individuals who are entering the workplace with the ability to attract groups of followers by demonstrating expertise in the social networking software realm (Hamel, 2009). The nine essential rules for Generation F leaders according to Hamel (2009) are as follows:

1. All ideas compete on an equal footing.

2. Contributions count for more than credentials.

3. Hierarchies are natural, not prescribed.

4. Leaders serve rather than preside.

5. Groups are self-defining and self-organizing.

6. Resources get attracted, not allocated.

7. Power comes from sharing information, not hoarding it.

8. Opinions compound and decisions are peer-reviewed.

9. Tasks are chosen, not assigned. (p. 1)

Social networking technologies such as weblogs (blogs) and video weblogs on sites such as DIGG, de.licio.us, Facebook, MySpace, Twitter, YouTube, and Flickr inspire individuals to participate in the social networking realm based on this new protocol.

Social networking software is a communication tool used to build communities of people who (a) share tacit knowledge skills, (b) share common beliefs, and (c) influence viewers by using storytelling techniques as a vehicle for communication (G. Solomon & Schrum, 2007). Although the original purpose of social networking software was for home computing by users between the ages of 12 and 18 years old, the use of social software in business environments by a different demographic of end users continues to rise (McGiboney, 2009). Since 2004, the use of social networking software has increased exponentially (McGiboney, 2009). Facebook has more than 200 million active users, and more than half of the users are out of college. The fastest growing demographic is those 35 years old and older. During the period between June 2008–June 2009, Twitter site visits increased 1,382%. The largest age group on Twitter is 35 to 49 years old, with nearly 3 million unique visitors comprising almost 42% of the site's audience (McGiboney, 2009).

SOCIAL NETWORKING: A LEADERSHIP PHENOMENON

The advent of social networking software has resulted in new types of leaders to emerge that were previously unknown, but gain popularity through the collective power of the group at the grassroots level. The ability to gain popularity as a leader using social networking software as a campaign tool was a key factor in the presidential victory of Barack Obama, who invigorated the world of politics by delivering a variety of compelling messages using a variety of social networking software (Navarsartian, 2008). Not only could voters passively read pertinent information about the candidate, but they could also contribute information and exchange feelings regarding political platforms using social networking software, which helped inspire a variety of new voters, especially those in the 18- to 24-year-old range (Navarsartian, 2008). The new paradigm of communication that has yielded phenomenal results in leadership effectiveness warrants further exploration as the use of social networking software continues to grow exponentially.

HARNESSING THE POWER OF
SOCIAL NETWORKING SITES FOR LEADERSHIP

Corporate leaders are still learning how to effectively communicate using social networking software tools because it is a relatively new technology medium, which can result in diminished leadership effectiveness, business expansion, and return on investment as many consumers are using social networking Web sites for business purposes (Bellamy, 2009; Elmore, 2009, C. Li & Bernoff, 2009; G. Solomon & Schrum, 2007). Leading companies use social networking sites as a *groundswell* to gain insights, generate revenue, energize customers, and save money, thereby leveraging the power of social networking communiqués (C. Li & Bernoff, 2009). In a leadership class at Baylor University, 73% of the students noted that they are using social networking Web sites such as Facebook, LinkedIn, and Twitter to search for jobs, as well as learn about companies that fit their career aspirations (Elmore, 2009). Companies that have a compelling presence by providing relevant and timely communications on social networking sites accelerate their business because they draw followers based on the ability to establish a personal connection (Elmore, 2009; Navarsartian, 2008). Because of the interest in this new mode of communications, the phenomenon of accelerated leadership and business growth using this technology is a fascinating topic that warrants further exploration.

Only a few previous studies were found that explore demonstrated leadership characteristics using social networking applications such as Facebook, Twitter, and YouTube (Bellamy, 2009; Elmore, 2009; C. Li & Bernoff, 2009). Some research studies have assessed and compiled statistics that find relationships between followers and friends, along with the tracking of emergent leaders on social networking platforms (Ferreira, 2009; Java, 2008, Y. Li, Tan, Teo, & Mattar, 2006; Navarsartian, 2008; Parr, 2009; G. Solomon & Schrum, 2007). However, limited studies exist in which researchers have explored the content of top-ranking leader accounts using a social networking software tool such as Twitter to find emergent patterns and themes based on prominent transactional and transformational leadership characteristics and are limited to Web sites that track general patterns and usage statistics (WeFollow, 2009).

PREDOMINANT LEADERSHIP CHARACTERISTICS FOUND ON SOCIAL NETWORKING SITES

In this qualitative research study, the leadership characteristics of top-ranking users who use Twitter for business communications were explored to gain an understanding of thematic elements that can accelerate business growth (Leedy & Ormrod, 2005; Patton, 2004). The communications of individuals who have emerged on social networking sites as leaders warrant further exploration to understand and accommodate this new paradigm of emerging talent and help accelerate future business growth. Leaders will need to solve problems in the workplace based on demonstrating advanced social networking software skills to solve business problems, market products and services, and position organizations for accelerated growth (Hamel, 2009; G. Solomon & Schrum, 2007). The ability for leaders to emerge in social networking software realms is a phenomenon for which further research might lead to an understanding of how leadership characteristics have evolved as a result of this new technology.

Content was uploaded into NVivo8 software and explored from a sample of the user accounts on Twitter that are listed in the WeFollow directory home page as the top 100 ranking Twitter users because of the large number of followers they attract (WeFollow, 2009). Twitter assigns three specific designations to users: (a) followers (user accounts that subscribe to information feeds) and (b) following (information feeds from other designated user accounts; Twitter, 2009). Consumers on Twitter choose their followers based on personal interests and can subscribe to data feeds by following a specific user account (Twitter, 2009). WeFollow is a Twitter user directory that allows users to self-designate categories based on their interests and list themselves in the directory based on these groupings. A statistical count of both followers and following are available on each Twitter account home page and the WeFollow Twitter Directory (Twitter, 2009; WeFollow, 2009).

The data for the current study were taken from a sampling of the top 100 ranked user accounts that publicly communicate using the Twitter software application and are categorized as entrepreneurs in the WeFollow Twitter directory (WeFollow, 2009). These user accounts are considered leaders in the Twitter realm of users because of the large number of followers that they attract (Java, 2008; Twitter, 2009). Emergent themes regarding the leadership characteristics were found by exploring the data. The design for the study might lead other researchers to explore other phenomena regarding social networking software connections and interactions.

Research Questions

In the qualitative study, content from the top leaders who use Twitter social networking software for business communications was explored to find emergent themes regarding transformational leadership characteristics. The findings from the study might be used to build future research models that will help organizations become successful when expanding globally by using Twitter for business communications and by understanding thematic attractants for followers who use social networking software such as Twitter. Thus, the following research question drove this study: What common themes are found in the public content of leaders on social networking sites such as Twitter that represent the characteristics of transactional and transformational leadership?

Relevant Literature

An examination of the literature related to leadership revealed ample peer-reviewed publications and other suitable print sources justifying the resource feasibility of the study. Scholars have previously approached the topic of consumer behavior theory and its applicability to business leadership although not from the perspective proposed in the current research (J. Aaker, 1997; D. A. Aaker & Joachimstaler, 2000). Transactional and transformational leadership characteristics are in a variety of studies in which researchers explore and assess traditional business leadership communications, but limited studies were found that explored the characteristics of top-ranking leaders using social networking software such as Twitter.

Consumer Behavior Theory

Leveraging brand names is a primary element of global strategy (J. Aaker, 1997; D. A. Aaker & Joachimstaler, 2000; Ballantyne, Warren, & Nobbs, 2006; Ferreira, 2007; Holt, 2004; Kim, 2004; M. R. Solomon, 2002). Understanding consumer perceptions is necessary to recognize accelerated business growth by effectively marketing in a virtual, global market (Ferreira, 2007). As indicated by consumer behavior theory, essential elements must be present to sell a product (J. Aaker, 1997; D. A. Aaker & Joachimstaler, 2000; M. R. Solomon, 2002). According to J. Aaker (1997), five core dimensions of a brand exist: (a) sincerity, (b) excitement, (c) competence, (d) sophistication, and (e) ruggedness. Brand personality might be used to investigate the status of a brand and predict the future state of the brand (J. Aaker, 1997; D. A. Aaker & Joachimstaler, 2000; Solomon, 2002). Consumers have many choices; therefore, the choice of a brand can also be applied to the concept of attracting followers on a social networking software medium such as Twitter as a vehicle for corporate marketing and business communications (Gartner, 2009; Hamel, 2009; G. Solomon & Schrum, 2007).

Consumers Are Followers

Consumers follow leaders on social networking sites based on the primary tenets of consumer behavior theory (G. Solomon & Schrum, 2007). However, the phenomenon of what attracts consumers to particular leaders who use social networking sites for communications has still not been determined. The phenomenon regarding what attracts consumers to leaders in industry by exploring positive branding messages found in corporate websites has been explored in current research, along with thematic elements found in specific communiqués (Ferreira, 2007; Hamel, 2009; Taylor, 2008). Taylor (2008) revealed that consumers with an interdependent self-understanding were partial to a transactional leader response, while consumers with an independent outlook favored a transformational response. Individuals who use social networking for business communications are autonomous, and therefore would be more attracted to leaders who are transformational than leaders who are transactional (Hamel, 2009).

Transactional Leadership

Transactional leadership models originate from a social exchange perspective that focuses on the implicit social contract between leaders and followers and its relationship to effectiveness (Avolio, 1999; Avolio & Bass, 1999). Typically, transactional models focus on exchange theory and the perceptions and expectations followers have regarding the actions and motives of leaders. Transactional leadership skills are necessary in the social networking paradigm, as the ability to send and receive information is a two-way exchange with leaders and followers exchanging communiqués in real time (Y. Li et al., 2006). According to Bass (1990), transactional leadership is a quid pro quo method with two dimensions: active management by exception (proactive leadership), and passive management by exception (reactive leadership). Because the intrinsic nature of transactional leadership communications is objective, the ability to identify and connect with the consumer audience is lacking due to the reliance on this type of leadership characteristic in a social networking realm (J. Aaker, 1997; Bass, 1990; M. R. Solomon, 2002).

Transformational Leadership

Transformational leadership supplements transactional leadership by building an emotional, inspirational appeal to followers that elevates performance and nurtures individual potential (Avolio, Bass, & Jung, 1999; Bass, 1990; Bass & Avolio, 1994; Y. Li et al., 2006). While early research on transformational leadership focused on the needs of leaders, the realm of transformational leadership was expanded in later research studies by making a stronger connection to followers' emotional needs (Bass, 1985, 1990; Bass & Avolio, 1994; Burns, 1978; Hater & Bass, 1998; Hunt & Conger, 1999).

Transformational leaders are able to get respondents to do much more then they had anticipated in an effort to satisfy the expectations of the leader (Bass, 1990).

Transformational leadership attributes noted in the results of research included an interest in emulating the leader, increased innovation, better overall performance, increased commitment, and improved self-confidence (Bass, 1985). Qualities of transformational leaders include idealized behavior (charisma), inspirational motivation (shared goal expression and understanding of good morals and ethics), intellectual stimulation (promotions of new ways of thinking), and individualized consideration (provision of individualized care and consideration; Bass, 1990; Y. Li et al., 2006). A transactional leader defines rules that outline what can be gained or lost by engaging in certain sets of actions (Bass, 1990).

Current Research on Transactional and Transformational Leadership

The motivation for Open Source Software (OSS) leaders to interact efficiently in a work environment related to transformational and transactional leadership traits in several leading research studies (Y. Li et al., 2006). Transformational leadership characteristics positively relate to developers' intrinsic motivation, and leaders' active management by exception, a form of transactional leadership characteristics, positively relates to developers' extrinsic motivation (Y. Li et al., 2006). The exploration of data to uncover thematic elements of both transactional and transformational leadership characteristics is pertinent to gaining a competitive leadership advantage on social networking sites such as Twitter.

Consumers are attracted to leaders who interact in a participatory global network exchange based on basic tenets of consumer behavior theory (J. Aaker, 1997; Ballantyne et al., 2006; Ferreira, 2007; Holt, 2004; Kim, 2004; M. R. Solomon, 2002). Transactional leaders evolve into transformational leaders by using bidirectional exchanges of information that inspire followers using inspiration and emotion (Bass, 1990; Y. Li et al., 2006; Woods, 2007). Transformational and transactional leadership skills can be used to influence viewers to engage in a social network community (G. Solomon & Schrum, 2007). Content from leaders on social networking sites can be explored in social networking communiqués to understand the phenomenon of the specific communication attractants found in the text that fit into the characteristics of transactional and transformational leadership.

Research Method

In this study, the textual content of the top-ranking leaders on Twitter was explored to find meanings embedded in a set of common words that are unique and specific to transactional and transformational leadership characteristics (Frankl, 1984). An understanding based on the beliefs and values of authors of peer-reviewed, journal articles was established, and qualitative content analysis research was determined to be an appropriate method for finding emergent patterns and themes in the data (Krippendorff, 1980). Text is quantified and tallied in a content analysis, which is a technique used to gather and analyze the content (Leedy & Ormrod, 2005) by relational and thematic analyses. In qualitative research, researchers are not interested in quantifying or validating causal relationships. The primary interest is to explore patterns by establishing meaning and themes of an incident's phenomena (Creswell, 2004; Krippendorff, 1980).

By exploring patterns of communication on Twitter using qualitative data analysis, information was gathered regarding the interpretation of a message by a test population (Chu, 1995). In the domain of social networking applications, the study of leadership core competencies is relevant because it can determine how constructed interpretations of messages embedded within the content of social networking software converge into similar themes that might explain their popularity on this new communication medium.

To begin the content analysis, the data content from the designated top-ranking Twitter accounts were saved as text files and then imported into the NVivo8 software for further categorization and analysis (QSR International, 2009). Multiple sources of data from different user accounts, including researcher notes, were collected and analyzed from the content to ensure validity of the research findings (Creswell, 2004; Denzin & Lincoln, 2005; Shadish, Cook, & Campbell, 2002; Trochim, 2006). The data were analyzed for emergent core themes, characteristics, and descriptions using a systematic content analysis methodology for coding data into common themes and terms (Neuendorf, 2002; Patton, 2004; Pennebaker & Chung, 2007). Similarities between meanings found in social networking software data grouped participant responses into common data categories based on the use of a single word. Because communications on Twitter are limited to 140 characters, the token of a single word rather than a phrase was a more appropriate choice. A total of 34,189 words were analyzed in the collection of data taken during the time period of 1 month from top-ranking Twitter accounts using NVivo8 software. The top 20 words were chosen that had the highest repetitive occurrence in the data using a reliability figure calculated using the methodology from a study recommended by Krippendorff titled *Computerized Text Analysis of Al-Quaeda Transcripts using the* co-occurrence of high-frequency content words (Pennebaker & Chung, 2007). The words were analyzed and grouped into thematic elements using the meaning extraction method used by Pennebaker and Chung (2007) with a *calculated percentage loading factor of 0.25 or higher* (see Table 1).

The study gained internal and external validity by using diverse data gathering and analysis processes (Creswell, 2004; Shadish et al.,

2002; Trochim, 2006; Trochim & Donnelly, 2008). The search for the perceived meaning of the data explored on successful social networking accounts resulted in an understanding of the phenomenon through data analysis (Pennebaker & Chung, 2007; Trochim & Donnelly, 2008). The results of the data analysis in the next section lead to conclusions and recommendations to finalize the study.

TABLE 1. *THEMATIC ELEMENTS OF CONTENT FOUND ON TOP TWITTER ACCOUNTS*

Theme	Categories	Words
Emotions	Positive	care
		feeling; funny
		happy
		health
		hope
		like
		lol (laugh out loud); love
	Negative	hunger
		want
	Neutral	feminine
Collaboration	Positive	give
		take
		organize
		connect
		friends
Action	Positive	change
		know
		think

RESULTS

The purpose of this qualitative study was to explore the communiqués of leaders who use the Twitter social networking software to find thematic elements that relate and expand upon the characteristics of transformational leadership. Content included text, hyperlinks, images, and video logs found embedded in the personal communications of the top-ranking Twitter users who have the highest statistical number of followers. A qualitative content analysis methodology extrapolated themes from the data. The research culminated in results based on the following research question: What common themes are found in the public content of social networking sites such as Twitter that represent the characteristics of transactional and transformational leadership?

The researcher explored perceptions, feelings, and meanings derived from all data sources, which included the content embedded in public Twitter accounts, including text, hyperlinks, images, and video logs. Results were grouped into separate text files for each Twitter user and uploaded into NVivo8 for analysis (QSR International, 2009). The data were grouped by uncovering patterns of repetitive word use. Recurring words that appeared in the content were extracted and regrouped into similar categories based on the meaning of the word. Thematic elements emerged based on the analyses (see Table 1 opposite).

The composite description describes the quintessence of transformational leadership characteristics found in the communiqués of leaders using Twitter social networking software. The researcher discontinued adding data to the analysis when saturation occurred and further analysis would produce redundant results (Creswell, 2004). A codebook was created by using the NVivo8 software tool that summarized references of words found in the consolidated content using mean percentages of total words per text file (Pennebaker &

Chung, 2007; see also Table 1). Three core themes emerged from the research data that resulted in the summarized composite description for the research study: (a) emotions, (b) collaboration, and (c) action (see Table 2).

TABLE 2. TRANSACTIONAL AND TRANSFORMATIONAL LEADERSHIP CHARACTERISTICS OF TWITTER USERS

Thematic Element	Transactional Leadership Characteristics	Transformational Leadership Characteristics
Emotions	Active exception	Individualized consideration
Collaboration	Active exception, passive exception	Intellectual stimulation
Action	Passive exception	Idealized behavior, inspirational motivation, intellectual stimulation, individualized consideration

Emotions

Leaders who use Twitter social networking software for business communiqués use words that illustrate different types of positive and negative emotions. Transformational leaders expand their realm by making a strong connection to their followers by uncovering the emotional needs of their followers, which is categorized as individual consideration (Bass, 1985, 1990). Two-way dialogue regarding personal emotions uses transactional leadership techniques (proactive leadership), and the subsequent content of the responses from the followers regarding emotions was inspired based on the transformational leadership characteristic of individual consideration that the leader gave to each follower, which demonstrated empathy for shared feelings.

Collaboration

Collaboration is a bidirectional exchange that follows the basic tenets of transactional leadership theory relating to both active and passive exception (Bass, 1990). Leaders engaged followers in a two-way conversation that could require direct action on the part of the leader to develop a response to the follower or could inspire other followers to respond, which would then delegate the leadership role to another user and require no further intervention from the leader. The specific characteristic of transformational leadership found in the thematic element of collaboration was intellectual stimulation. Collaboration is a new skill that leaders must engage in to foster intellectual stimulation to experience growth using transformational leadership characteristics (Bass, 1985, 1990; Hamel, 2009). The continuum of communications using social networking software tools such as Twitter depends on leaders to inspire followers to continue in a two-way, horizontal exchange of information. The ability to attract more followers by stimulating additional discussions on a specific topic presented by the leader expands the sphere of influence by gaining an expanded set of followers through the new set of connections (Java, 2008).

Action

The leaders used words that resulted in a call to action to their followers that were emotional but directive rather than passive. The ability to inspire and motivate followers into action was a final important theme found in the data. This thematic element included the transactional leadership qualities of passive exception. Two-way dialogue was established using transactional techniques, and the subsequent content of the responses from the followers were inspired based on transformational leadership characteristics found embedded in the message. Leaders inspired followers into action based on their charismatic persona, inspirational message, promotion of new techniques, and demonstration of care and consideration for each follower in the two-way dialogue found in the data. Leaders used action words intended to inspire transactional and transformational leadership characteristics as described by Bass (1990) by inspiring social change through compelling messages sent via communiqués using Twitter social networking software.

A synergistic transformational leadership model follows the movements of the thematic elements based on their interactions (see Figure 1). Emotional words inspired followers to respond to the message, thus inspiring collaboration. Collaboration continued between the leader and the follower in a dynamic two-way exchange that resulted in action. Emotions also can result in direct calls to action in a social networking environment. This cyclical transactional and transformational leadership model embodies the ideal set of interactions in a social networking environment.

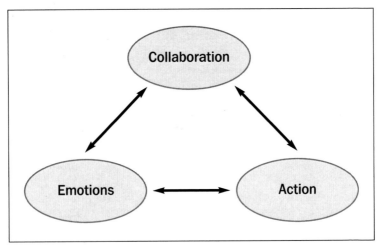

Figure 1. Social networking transformational model.

SUMMARY AND CONCLUSIONS

This final section presents an overview of the research study findings, focusing on the research question. The three major core themes created in the research study are reiterated to illustrate the key findings for the qualitative content analysis study. Interpretations of the findings and impacts on leadership, inferences, study recommendations, and future research recommendations are revealed. The research question that directed the study was as follows: What common themes are found in the public content of social networking sites such as Twitter that represent the characteristics of transactional and transformational leadership? The findings are important because followers are attracted to leaders based on the basic tenets of consumer behavior theory coupled with transactional and transformational leadership characteristics that inspire existing followers and generate new connections (J. Aaker, 1997, Java, 2008; M. R. Solomon, 2002). Followers are merely consumers found in the new realm of social networking, where communiqués occur in real time and information is fleeting and transitory (Java, 2008). Common terms and themes converge into patterns of consumer use that summarize specific content found on social networking sites such as Twitter. An exploration of content found on social networking sites such as Twitter extends research by providing a qualitative analysis regarding why consumers choose to engage with a specific person on a social networking software site based on demonstrated transactional and transformational leadership skills.

Transactional leadership tenets allow leaders to engage followers using passive and active exceptions in two-way exchanges of information, which result in either explicit or delegated action from the leader to the follower (Bass, 1990). Transformational leadership elevates the performance of workers by following a specific set of characteristics. Characteristics of transformational leaders include idealized behavior, inspirational motivation, intellectual stimulation, and individualized consideration (Bass, 1990).

Three predominant themes emerged that described elements of the communiqués based on the clustering of similar words found in the data: (a) emotions, (b) collaboration, and (c) action (see Table 1). The thematic elements demonstrate specific transactional and transformational leadership characteristics found in the personal communications of top-ranking users using the Twitter social networking tool (see Table 2). A synergistic, cyclical transactional and transformational leadership model embodies the quintessence of interactions in a social networking environment (see Figure 1).

Although the content analysis and thematic analysis of the data described the demonstrated leadership characteristics found in the consolidated content of the communiqués, the individual aptitudes of each leader are unknown and require follow-on research using an instrument such as the Multifactor Leadership Questionnaire (Antonakis, Avolio, & Sivasubramaniam, 2003; Avolio & Bass, 1999; Avolio et al., 1995). It was not known whether followers engage in actions prescribed by the top-ranking users on social networking sites, nor did the study explore or assess the outcome of the actions if they were taken. The only absolute conclusion from this research study was that top-ranking users on Twitter exercise certain words that have thematic elements of transactional and transformational leadership, as indicated by the high number of statistical rankings for each word. Future research might include an exploration and examination of the usefulness of the messages transmitted using social networking tools.

References

Aaker, D. A., & Joachimstaler, E. (2000). *Building strong brands.* New York, NY: Free Press.

Aaker, J. (1997). Dimension of brand personality. *Journal of Marketing Research, 34,* 347–356.

Antonakis, J., Avolio, B. J., & Sivasubramaniam, N. (2003). Context and leadership: An examination of the nine-factor full range leadership theory using the Multifactor Leadership Questionnaire. *The Leadership Quarterly, 14,* 261–295.

Avolio, B. J. (1999). *Full leadership development: Building the vital forces in organizations.* Thousand Oaks, CA: Sage.

Avolio, B. J., & Bass, B. M. (1999). Re-examining the components of transformational and transactional leadership using the Multifactor Leadership Questionnaire. *Journal of Occupational & Organizational Psychology, 72,* 441–462.

Avolio, B. J., Bass, B. M., & Jung, D. I. (1995). *Multifactor Leadership Questionnaire technical report.* Redwood City, CA: Mind Garden.

Ballantyne, R., Warren, A., & Nobbs, K. (2006). The evolution of brand choice. *Journal of Brand Management, 13,* 339–352.

Bass, B. M. (1985). *Leadership and performance beyond expectation.* New York, NY: Free Press.

Bass, B. M. (1990). *Bass and Stodgill's handbook of leadership: Theory, research, and managerial applications* (3rd ed.). New York, NY: Free Press.

Bass, B. M., & Avolio, B. J. (1994). Shatter the glass ceiling: Women may make better managers. *Human Resources Management, 33,* 549–560.

Bellamy, K. (2009). Integral for the masses a fresh perspective on technology and its role in furthering integral leadership. *Integral Leadership Review, 9*(4), 1–5.

Burns, J. M. (1978). *Leadership.* New York, NY: Harper & Row.

Chu, S. (1995). *Cross cultural comparison of the perception of symbols* (Doctoral dissertation). Retrieved from ProQuest Digital Dissertations database. (UMI No. 9700924).

Creswell, J. W. (2004). *Planning, conducting, and evaluating quantitative and qualitative research* (3rd ed.). Columbus, OH: Merrill/Prentice Hall.

Denzin, N. K., & Lincoln, Y. S. (2005). *The Sage handbook of qualitative research* (3rd ed.). Thousand Oaks, CA: Sage.

Elmore, B. (2009). Social networking strategies. *Baylor Business Review, 28,* 25–27.

Ferreira, G. (2007). *Consumer perceptions of global branding and iconization.* (Doctoral dissertation). Retrieved from the ProQuest Digital Dissertations database. (UMI No. 3272246).

Ferreira, G. (2009, June). *Using social networking tools for research.* Paper presented at the Northcentral University annual instructional methodology meeting, Prescott Valley, AZ.

Frankl, V. E. (1984). *Man's search for meaning.* Riverside, NJ: Simon & Schuster.

Friedman, R. (2006). *The world is flat: A brief history of the twenty-first century.* New York, NY: Farrar, Straus, and Giroux.

Gartner. (2009). *Gartner: Insight and advice from 1000 technology experts.* Retrieved March 4, 2009, from www.gartner.com

Hamel, G. (2009). The Facebook generation versus the Fortune 500. Retrieved from http://blogs.wsj.com/management/2009/03/24/the-facebook-generation-vs-thefortune500/

Hater, J. J., & Bass, B. M. (1998). Superiors' evaluation and subordinates' perceptions of transformational and transactional leadership, *Journal of Applied Psychology, 73,* 695–702.

Holt, D. B. (2004). *How brands become icons.* Cambridge, MA: Harvard Business School Press.

Hunt, J. G., & Conger, J. A. (1999). From where we sit: An assessment of transformational and charismatic leadership research. *Leadership Quarterly, 10,* 335–343.

Java, A. (2008). Mining social media communities and content. (Doctoral dissertation). Retrieved from the ProQuest Digital Dissertations database. (UMI No. 3339175).

Kim, E. S. (2004). *The meanings of the global brand: A perspective from the*

Korean consumers. (Doctoral dissertation). Retrieved from the ProQuest Digital Dissertations database. (UMI No. 3139769).

Krippendorff, K. (1980). *Content analysis: An introduction to its methodology.* Beverly Hills, CA: Sage.

Leedy, P. D., & Ormrod, J. E. (2005). *Practical research: Planning and design* (8th ed.). Upper Saddle River, NJ: Prentice Hall.

Li, C., & Bernoff, J. (2008). *Groundswell: Living in a world transformed by social technologies.* Boston, MA: Harvard Business School.

Li, Y., Tan, C. H., Teo, H., & Mattar, A. T. (2006). *Motivating open source software developers: Influence of transformational and transactional leaderships.* Paper presented at proceedings of the 2006 ACM SIGMIS CPR conference on computer personnel research: Forty-four years of computer personnel research: achievements, challenges, and the future, Claremont, CA, USA. doi:10.1145/1125170.112582

McGiboney, M. (2009, March 18). Twitters tweet smell of success. Retrieved from http://blog.nielsen.com/nielsenwire/online_mobile/twitters-tweet-smell-of-success

Navarsartian, K. (2008). Digging for votes: An analysis of 2008 presidential candidates' use of new media. (Master's thesis). Retrieved from the ProQuest Digital Dissertations database. (UMI No. 1454074).

Neuendorf, K. (2002). *The content analysis guidebook.* Thousand Oaks, CA: Sage.

Parr, B. (2009). Five terrific Twitter research tools. Retrieved from http://mashable.com/2009/05/03/twitter-research-tools/

Patton, M. Q. (2004). *Qualitative research & evaluative methods.* London, UK: Sage.

Pennebaker, J. W., & Chung, C. K. (2007). Computerized text analysis of Al-Qaeda transcripts. In K. Krippendorff & M. Bock (Eds.), *A content analysis reader* (pp. 453–464). Thousand Oaks, CA: Sage.

QSR International. (2009). QSR home page. Retrieved from www.qsrinternational.com

Shadish, W. R., Cook, T. D., & Campbell, D. T. (2002). *Experimental and quasiexperimental designs for generalized causal inference.* Boston, MA: Houghton Mifflin.

Solomon, G., & Schrum, L. (2007). *Web 2.0: New tools, new schools.* Eugene, OR: International Society for Technology in Education.

Solomon, M. R. (2002). *Consumer behavior: Buying, having, and being* (5th ed.). Upper Saddle River, NJ: Prentice Hall.

Taylor, D. W. (2008). How self-construal affects consumer relations to unexpected events: The effects of event valence, event experience, event spread, and leadership intervention. (Unpublished Doctoral Dissertation). State University of New York at Binghamton, Binghamton, NY.

Trochim, W. M. K. (2006). *Qualitative validity.* Retrieved from www.social-researchmethods.net/kb/qualval.php

Trochim, W. M. K., & Donnelly, J. P. (2008). *The research methods knowledge base* (4th ed.). Mason, OH: Cengage Learning.

Twitter. (2009). Twitter home page. Retrieved from http://twitter.com

WeFollow. (2009). *Twitter directory and search: Find Twitter followers.* Retrieved from http://wefollow.com

About the Author

Dr. Gail Ferreira holds several nationally accredited degrees: a Bachelor of Science (BS) in Computer Science from National University; a Master of Science (MS) in Computer Science from National University; and a Doctor of Management (DM) from University of Phoenix, Phoenix, AZ.

Dr. Gail Ferreira is an educational and research technical expert who actively teaches for both industry and academia. She teaches and develops educational materials for a breadth of research, writing, and technical courses at an advanced level, having taught thousands of students in the last 5 years in both an online as well as a live learning environment.

In academia, she works with Walden University as an Associate Professor for the Doctorate of Business Administration program; and Northcentral University where she is the Applied Computing Science Lead, setting the pace for Northcentral Universities' Doctoral level course design and development. Dr. Gail is also on faculty with Strayer University, University of the Rockies, and University of Phoenix. Additionally, she acts as a committee chairperson for doctoral dissertation research, specializing in qualitative, quantitative, and mixed methodologies.

Dr. Gail is an independent technical solutions consultant and project manager, with expertise with enterprise software solutions including Vignette, Kronos, and Oracle.

To reach Dr. Gail Ferreira for information on any of these topics, please email: drgail.ferreira@gmail.com.

CHAPTER 9

Globalization of Body Language

Dr. Judy Fisher-Blando
Dr. T.G. Robinson
Dr. Cheryl A. Lentz

WORLD WITHOUT BORDERS

With easier travel, international media, and access to new information technology, globalization has recently become a defining buzzword in most cultures. Once, *international* was the appropriate way to explain the operations of multinational business. *Globalization* is the new term that describes interests and operations not only in most countries, but also in those operations that "functionally divide their activities in different countries, producing one part of a product here, another part there, assembling the elsewhere, marketing them throughout the world and controlling and coordinating all these activities from a home base" (De George, 2006, p. 537). Globalization is the process of interaction and integration among communities, organizations, and governments of different nations. This process "has an effect on the environment, on culture, on political systems, on economic development and prosperity, and on human physical well-being in societies around the world" (The Levin Institute, 2010, p. 1). Cultural communication, including how individuals define their local and communal identity, is the ways and methods members communicate with each other through body language. By extension, the global nature of intercultural communication is no longer an option, but a necessity for leaders and followers alike; good nonverbal communication skills are part of a progressive professional portfolio and a distinct advantage to those who can master the hidden messages of body language, the focus of this chapter.

According to Leavitt (2009)

> . . . the global corporation has replaced the multinational corporation as the most effective international competitor. The multinational corporation conducts its business in various countries, adapting its products and practices to local conditions by customizing products for specific markets. In contrast, the global corporation avoids the high relative costs of the multinational corporation by offering universal standardized productions for a homogeneous world market. (as cited in Gibson, Ivancevich, Donnelly, & Konopaske, 2009, p. 55)

Organizations are no longer constrained by borders. Even in local organizations, diversity encourages working with others who were born and raised in different *cultures,* more than simply foreign *countries.* Consequently, every decision requires the interpretation of verbal and nonverbal information through a variety of lenses.

According to Kottak and Kozaitis (2008) there exists a concept of transnational communities where "cultural patterns, loyalties, and social relations are regionally rooted but linked to [much] larger systems" (p. 66). According to Robinson (2008) communicating effectively and understanding body language within larger communities offers a new description of different nonverbal cues, which can cause less dissention when collaborating on a successful outcome using *thought diversity* or the mix of diverse perspectives based on cultural, intellectual, and cognitive variations. The failure to interpret correctly hidden dimension of body language for integration of thought diversity, dissenting points of view, and open group communications management is creating a crisis with technology leaders in decision-making roles (Tapscott & Williams, 2006; Teradata, 2004). "In a complex society like the United States or Canada, people constantly negotiate their social identities. All of us wear different hats, presenting ourselves sometimes as one thing, sometimes another" (Kottak & Kozaitis, 2008, p. 68) in which body language offers help in this communication.

Implementation of outdated decision-making protocols framed from consensus-building paradigms and lack of understanding of meta-communications nuisances, set in motion a ripple effect throughout organizations. The resulting outcomes were damage to public relations, viability, and survivability (Katz, 2003; Useem, 2004). The necessity to make the most of input from team members, stakeholders, and other decision influencers closest to the theater of operation or company workplace environment is critical to providing data that can be transformed into business intelligence and corporate knowledge (Schultz-Hardt, Mojzisch, Brodbeck, Kerschreiter, & Frey, 2006).

Global leaders of tomorrow must be multi-linguists and fluent in the *paralinguistic vocabularies* of Kinesics (communication by body movement) and Proxemics (communication by body position) in order to effectively decipher the increasingly higher rates of bi-directional flow of information (Teradata, 2004). International *knowledge workers* operate in the age of data proliferation, in which only partial and limited information, albeit in massive volumes, is available. Contained within the non-sequenced *Petabyte packets* of information are non-correlated *second-order messages* that can significantly affect the efficiency of decision-making outcomes (Teradata, 2004). Ultimately, post-modern leadership is about effective communications and creating an inclusive environment for an exchange of ideas and sustained dialogue.

Goals of Communication

Communication is the process of sending and receiving symbols, and messages with attached meanings (Schermerhorn, Hunt, & Osborn, 2008). Meanings and interpretations may vary among different cultures however. Mixed messages that give confused or conflicting verbal and nonverbal cues may interfere with efficient communication. Efficient communication across cultures includes understanding the exact meaning and intent of others, being understood, gaining acceptance for one's self and for ideas, and producing action or change. Obvious nonverbal listening behaviors mostly used are: making eye contact, being expressive and alert, moving closer to the speaker, active and mindful listening, use of facial expressions, touch, space, and use of time (Schermerhorn et al., 2008).

Barriers such as those outlined above can influence efficient communication. Selective perceptions, information overload, emotions, gender differences, and the act of being politically correct can distort communication and body language. Filtering can occur when there are differences in status. When verbal and nonverbal information exceeds human processing capacity, the result is information overload. How a person receiving nonverbal signals at the time of receipt influences interpretation. Men and women tend to gesture in different ways to show emotions. Finally, politically correct communication is more concerned with not being offensive that can cause a loss of free nonverbal expression (Robbins & Judge, 2009). Ambiguous communications and cultural differences can affect the capacity of the receiver's interpretations and effective decision-making. According to Gibson, Ivancevich, Donnelly, and Konopaske (2009) "manager[s] will have to study socialization much more closely and intervene so that the maximum benefits result from hiring [and working with] an increasingly diverse workforce" (p. 48).

Investing in the social capital of diversity—learning to more effectively work with others on a variety of different levels is an important element of the constantly shifting global landscape. "Socializing an ethnically diverse workforce is a two-way proposition. Not only must the manager learn about the employees' cultural background, but the employee must also learn about the rituals, customs, and values of the firm or work unit" (Gibson et al., p. 49) as well. Much more of a broader focus is needed to sustain a competitive advantage. Instead, "using the multi-cultural workforce to better compete, penetrate, and succeed in foreign cultures is one potential benefit of managing diversity effectively" (Gibson et al., p. 49).

Another aspect of the globalization and power of body language in cultures is the proliferation of conference calls versus face-to-face sessions. According to Robinson (2008) video conference calls, recognized as the primary way of conducting business in many of today's business sectors, and face-to-face session, considered more of a luxury, especially in the global workplace, present unique opportunities for sending and receiving nonverbal queues. The knowledge transfer between diverse team members in these two primary areas of data transmission is an important facet of information interpretation in multi-generation technology environments. This becomes crucial to select the most important tool for the most effective outcome.

For example, the most effective ways to communicate with the Baby Boomer generation (members born between 1946 and 1964) are not the same ways to interact with Generation X (members born between 1965 and 1980) or Generation Y (members born between 1981 and 1994. Generation X members prefer video conference calls and web conferencing to in-person meetings, especially for collaborative actions. Face-to-face meetings require, a small productive group, attuned to nonverbal signals. Generation Y members also are not shy about sending direct nonverbal signals, leveraged to promote *listening to understand* collaboration and knowledge sharing (Auby, 2008).

The essence of communicating effectively in a global environment is for all participants in the paralinguistic information exchange to tune-in on cultural specific sensory perceptions associated with the ability to receive and derive information from specific nonverbal components (Brislin, 2000). For example, seat positioning, voice pauses, and body language are especially important as group decision-making teams are in their forming stages (LaRue, Childs, & Larson, 2004). The interpretation of sensory perceptions is essential to fostering an inclusive dialogue and harnessing the authority and influence created by unconscious signals esoterically conveyed by different global cultures.

Power and Persuasion of Body Language

Body language is the nonverbal communication using facial expressions, eye behavior, gestures, posture, tone of voice, even small movements barely perceptible such as a shrug of the shoulder or nod of the head. Body language expresses feelings, emotion, and attitudes, and can contradict the messages conveyed by spoken language (Abrante, 2006; Henley, 1977). Statistics estimate that 60% to 90% of communication is nonverbal (Henley). Nonverbal messages can be more powerful than words, so it is important to focus on body cues during interactions. People in all cultures understand some nonverbal expressions; other expressions are particular to specific cultures. The lack of understanding body language throughout different cultures can lead to confusion and misunderstandings. Even the simplest gestures can have different meanings in different countries.

According to Gibson et al., (2009) there exists a national culture

> . . . a set of values, attitudes, beliefs, and norms shard by a majority of the inhabitants of a country . . . People in a society learn what to nice and what not to notice, how to behave

with each other, and how to handle responsibility, success, and failure. Most people are unaware of just how their culture has influenced their values, attitudes, beliefs, and norms (p. 61) that are often conveyed well beyond words.

A common mistake during team formation and decision-making is the intentional exclusion of different-minded thinkers or decision participants who use dissimilar qualitative, quantitative, or symbolic thought paradigms to processes decision criteria, raw data, and other intelligence. However, by including a globally, gender diverse and cognitively cross-functional team, the potential for misinterpretations of synchronous verbal/ nonverbal *clusters* and the exchanges of *payloads* of multiple-meanings can mitigate the value of forming diverse, multi-dimensional team that have the respect from other members of the organizational community, positional power or influence within the organization, leadership skills, and a team-oriented approach to problem solving (LaRue, Childs, & Larson, 2004). Bolman and Deal (2003) stated, "When a group encounters the individual vicissitudes of group life, such things as overloads, conflict, confusion, communications gaps, or bungled handoffs" (p. 109), the group has an opportunity to re-direct these unexpected changes into a positive frame. By re-framing, negative energy caused by misinterpretations of body language and other nonverbal components, a leader can channel the cross-group dynamics to create positive change and transformational action despite a team's national, social, or ethnic dissimilarities.

Maxwell (1998) stated that, "the true meaning of leadership is influence, nothing more, nothing less" (p. 11). The influence of a group leader's pre-decision preferences in selecting a course of action can either position the corporate entity for future success or failure (Brodbeck, Kerschreiter, Mojzisch, Frey, & Schulz-Hardt, 2002). A decision-maker's influence extends to the ability to foster a decision-making dialogue that facilitates open discussion and shared learning. The Thought Leadership approach depends on respectful and purposeful inquiry, enhancing group awareness of individual and team contributions to the decision-making dialogue and a fluent understanding of the interaction between components of in-depth and genuine communication (Somerville, Schader, & Huston, 2005). What type of leader are you and are you aware of the differences in paralinguistic interpretation around the globe?

Cultural Differences

Cultural differences in body language may show up in a wide variety of ways, as in a handshake, a nod of the head, or tone of voice. Some cultures are very expressive with physical touch whereas other cultures require a more comfortable distance. Italians consider a big hug and kiss on each cheek a common and acceptable greeting, compared to Japan in which a proper greeting consists of a respectful bow and no touch at all. Global diversity as well as the practical implications of working cross-culturally involves differences based on communication and body language variations and meanings.

United States and Canada

In the United States and Canada, a firm handshake is acceptable as a salutation and nonverbal contract. In Western cultures, people make intermittent eye contact while speaking to demonstrate interest and trustworthiness. North Americans usually smile automatically when greeting others, whereas people from other cultures may interpret this as insincere. The amount of personal space North Americans require is about the length of an arm (Weng, 2010). Although usually shaking one's head from side-to-side indicates 'no' in many countries, this simple gesture does not have a universal meaning.

Europe and Asia

Germans give a firm handshake. Men traditionally accompany the handshake with a slight bow. Germans and Japanese need more space. The size of one's personal space is influenced by social status, gender, age, and other factors. Many people from Asian cultures bow in greeting. Thais bow with their palms together and fingers outstretched, whereas people from Cambodia and Laos bow with their hands in front of their chests (Weng, 2010).

In Japan, a handshake is with a fully extended arm, accompanied by a bow. In Japan, people bow with their hands at their sides, and the depth of the bow is related to the level of respect because of the other person. Pakistanis use the *salaam,* and bow with the palm of the right hand on their foreheads. However, in Japan direct eye contact is interpreted as an invasion of a person's privacy and an act of rudeness. For instance, if a person is lost in Japan that person is much more likely to receive help from a local citizen if the person shows respectful body language and follows local customs of bowing and avoiding touch. Japanese smile less than Westerners, and in Korea it is considered inappropriate for adults to smile in public. For Koreans, a smile usually indicates embarrassment and not pleasure (Goman, 2008; Reiman, 2007; Varner & Beamer, 2004; Weng, 2010).

People from southern India and Pakistan move their head from side to side to express a variety of meanings. Depending on the context, this headshake could indicate 'you're welcome,' 'goodbye,' enjoyment, the equivalent of a shrug, or that the person acknowledges what another person has said. Bulgarians shake their head to indicate agreement. In France, a soft, quick handshake is offered. The French, Latin Americans, and Arabs need less personal space (Goman, 2008; Reiman, 2007; Varner & Beamer, 2004).

Middle East

In the Middle East, a handshake is given with the free hand placed on the forearm of the other person. People in the Middle East use very intense and prolonged eye contact to gauge someone else's intentions, and will move in very close to see the other person's eyes better. In the Middle East, pointing the bottom of one's foot (showing the sole) in another person's direction is extremely offensive, as is sitting cross-legged considered an insult. In the Middle East a male businessperson has much more leeway in terms of in which and how he walks than a female does, not to mention much different levels of access to local business opportunities. Fewer women do business in the Middle East because the cultural aversion to interacting with women is just too much to overcome. For the Maori of New Zealand, a traditional greeting "includes the pressing together the noses (the *hongi*) and a cry of welcome (the *karanga*)" (Weng, 2010, p. 1).

Decision-making Using Body Language

An increasing number of organizations use decision-making groups for decision-making functions (Keuffel, 2004). The evolving decision-making role of the groups necessitates the development of emerging decision-making strategies and deeper understanding of nonverbal communications to improve quality of judgments, timeliness of decisions, and consideration of dissenting, contradictory evidence, and data (Bazerman & Chugh, 2006; Sanfey, 2007). This heightened need to become more effective conveyers and listeners of nonverbal communications is essential for creating constructs that frame decision-making processes based on unbiased cognitive paradigms; and will benefit current and future leaders by facilitating more informed and timely decisions (Macpherson, 2007; Osman & Stavy, 2006).

Body language is an important part of communication in all cultures. By reading and interpreting body language, one can predict and persuade other people's mood and thinking processes. One's own body language can persuade decision-making by using gestures in harmony with his or her present state or mood. According to Borg (2009) effective persuasion combines equal parts communication and observation. Effective persuasion hinges on possessing good people skills, being able to read people, being a good and empathetic listener.

Because important decisions in business, politics, education, health, and culture can affect citizens of more than one nation, it is crucial that communication between people of different nations must be effective and all parties should emerge with the same understanding. Acknowledging and understanding the body language of different cultures allows people to make decisions who are more rational. A deeper understanding of the vast system of symbols and emblematic behaviors is critical to international success, because global leaders operate in increasingly diverse and complex global networks and in decision-making environments that require an increased number of time-bounded interactions with a wider range of stakeholders and systems (Schaub, 2003).

Future generations will be perceptive and well-informed in the exploration of the participative group decision-making processes and protocols (Schulz-Hardt et al., 2006). In an attempt to improve the quality of decisions, an increased awareness of existing real-world perceptions of body language, especially reflecting a dissenting or counter-intuitive position, could precipitate cognitive models that cultivate a combined constructive conflict and consensus-building approach to decision-making (Roberto, 2005).

CONCLUSION

This chapter provided an overview of the persuasion and power of body language and intercultural communication through globalization. Leaders must understand not only how nonverbal actions will affect crucial decisions, but also the significant impact nonverbal trends have on communication and decision-making. Whether working in a diverse organization or traveling to other countries for business or pleasure, one must know how the wrong body language can effect communication. Using the wrong gestures can cause cancelled business deals hostile and dangerous situations. Knowledge of different body language nuances is fundamental to diverse and effective communication. Learning expectations of other cultures shows a respect for the culture, a respect for the members of its communities, and may protect a visitor from inadvertently breaking a law.

Global leaders of tomorrow face a myriad of issues that include group decision-makers following a majority-rules process paradigm based on shared preferences and potentially missing critical data input because of the paradoxical nature of sending and receiving nonverbal queues during the decision-making process (Dooley & Fryxell, 1999). To survive and succeed in the new global community, leaders must master the art of operating in a diverse and complex decision-making environment, in which increased interactions require innovative solutions to address technical, financial, staffing challenges by harnessing the power of understanding Body language within an international context.

A combination of improved understanding on nonverbal components, inclusive group leadership styles that value diversity of thought (and thought leadership), will create new wave global business cultures that encourage constructive conflict in a shared information forum and are sensitive to the syntax and semantics of a heightened dialogue (Keuffel, 2004; Roberto, 2005; Schulz-Hardt et al., 2006). The leaders and followers, who learn to convey their message via symbols, signs, and emotionally intelligent behavior and decode the abstract nature of body posture, gestures, and facial signs, will be the select few who will provide the innovative solution that fuel the future engine of globalization and change.

References

Auby, K. (2008, August 25). A Boomer's guide to communicating with Gen X and Gen Y. *Business Week, 4097,* 63. Retrieved from EbscoHost database.

Bazerman, M., & Chugh, D. (2006). Decisions without blinders. *Harvard Business Review, 84*(1), 88–97. Retrieved from EbscoHost database.

Bolman, L., & Deal, T. (2003). *Reframing organizations: Artistry, choice, and leadership* (3rd ed.). San Francisco: Jossey-Bass.

Borg, J. (2009). *Persuasion: The art of influencing people.* FT Press.

Brislin, R. (2000). *Understanding culture's influence on behavior* (2nd ed.). New York: Harcourt College Publishers.

Brodbeck, F., Kerschreiter, R., Mojzisch, A., Frey, D., & Schulz-Hardt, S. (2002). The dissemination of critical, unshared information in decision-making groups: the effects of pre-discussion dissent. *European Journal of Social Psychology, 32*(1), 35–56. Retrieved from EbscoHost database.

De George, R. T. (2006). *Business ethics* (6th ed.). Upper Saddle River, NJ: Prentice Hall.

Dooley, R., & Fryxell, G. (1999). Attaining decision quality and commitment from dissent: The Moderating effects of loyalty and competence in strategic decision-making teams. *Academy of Management Journal, 42*(4), 389–402. Retrieved from EbscoHost database.

Gibson, J., Ivancevich, J., Donnelly, Jr., J., & Konopaske, R. (2009). *Organizations: Behavior, structure, processes* (13th ed.). New York: McGraw Hill.

Goman, C. (2008). *The nonverbal advantage: Secrets and science of body language at work.* Berrett-Koehler Publishers.

Henley, N. (1977). *Body politics-power, sex and nonverbal communication.* London: Prentice-Hall.

Katz, R. (2003). *The human side of managing technological innovation* (2nd ed.). New York: Oxford University Press.

Keuffel, W. (2004). Find your voice. *Software Development, 12*(9), 96. Retrieved from EbscoHost database.

Kottak, C. P., & Kozaitis, K. A. (2009). *On being different: Diversity and multiculturalism in the North American mainstream* (3rd ed.). Boston: McGraw Hill.

LaRue, B., Childs, P., & Larson, K. (2004). *Leading organizations from the inside out: Unleashing the collaborative genius of action-learning* teams. New York: John Wiley & Sons.

The Levin Institute (2010). *What is globalization?* www.globalization101.org/What_is_Globalization.html?PHPSESSID=07574b3da58ee5d4bf91e85d3c d2e580.

Macpherson, R. (2007). Cognitive ability, thinking dispositions, and instructional set as predictors of critical thinking. *Learning & Individual differences, 17*(2), 115–127. Retrieved from EbscoHost database.

Maxwell, W. T. (1998). *The 21 irrefutable laws of leadership.* Nashville, TN: Thomas Nelson, Inc.

Osman, M., & Stavy, R. (2006, December). Development of intuitive rules: Evaluating the application of the dual-system framework to understanding children's intuitive reasoning. *Psychonomic Bulletin & Review, 13*(6), 935–954. Retrieved from ProQuest database.

Reiman, T. (2007). *The power of body language.* Pocket Publishing.

Robbins, S. P., & Judge, T. A. (2009). *Organizational behavior* (13th ed.). Upper Saddle River, NJ: Pearson Prentice Hall.

Robinson, T. G. (2008). *A qualitative phenomenological evaluation of minority opinions in decision-making dialogues.* Unpublished doctoral dissertation, University of Phoenix.

Roberto, M. A. (2005). *Why great leaders don't take yes for an answer: Managing for conflict and consensus.* Upper Saddle River, NJ: Wharton School Publishing.

Sanfey, A. G. (2007). Decision neuroscience: New directions in studies of judgment and decision-making. *Current Directions in Psychological Science, 16*(3), 151–155 [Fordham electronic library]. Retrieved from ProQuest Blackwell Synergy database.

Schaub, L. (2003). Blocking made easy (or at least easier): Taking a look at the dynamics of dissent. *Communities, 119*(1), 6–8. Retrieved from EBSCO-host database.

Schermerhorn, J., Hunt, J., & Osborn, R. (2008). *Organizational behavior* (10th ed.). Hoboken, NJ: John Wiley & Sons.

Schulz-Hardt, S., Mojzisch, A., Brodbeck, F., Kerschreiter, R., & Frey, D. (2006). Group decision-making in hidden profile situations: Dissent as a facilitator for decision quality. *Journal of Personality and Social Psychology, 91*(6), 1080–1093. Retrieved from EbscoHost database

Somerville, M. M., Schader, B., & Huston, M. E. (2005). Rethinking what we do and how we do it: systems thinking strategies for library Leadership. *Australian Academic & Research Libraries, 36*(4), 214–228. Retrieved from General OneFile database.

Tapscott, D., & Williams, A. (2006). *Wikinomics: How mass collaboration changes everything.* New York: Penguin Group, Inc.

Teradata. (2004). *The 2003–2004 Teradata report on enterprise decision-making.* Retrieved from www.teradatalibrary.com

Useem, M. (2004). The essence of leading and governing deciding. In R. Gandossy & J. Sonnenfeld (Eds.), *Leadership and governance from the inside out* (pp. 117–122). Hoboken, NJ: John Wiley & Sons.

Varner, I., & Beamer, L. (2004). *Intercultural communication in the global workplace.* McGraw-Hill/Irwin.

Weng, S. (2010). *Body language across culture.* Retrieved from www.medhunters.com/articles/bodyLanguageAcrossCultures.html

About the Authors

Southern California author **Dr. Judy Fisher-Blando** holds several nationally accredited degrees: a Bachelor of Science (BS) in Business Management; a Master of Art in Organizational Management (MAOM); and a Doctorate of Management (DM) in Organizational Leadership from the University of Phoenix School of Advanced Studies.

Dr. Judy is also a faculty member for University of Phoenix and Walden University.

Dr. Judy is an expert in Value Stream Mapping, showing organizations how to 'lean' processes to eliminate non-value added tasks, which saves time, adds quality, and increases profits. She is also an expert on Workplace Bullying, having written her research dissertation on *Workplace Bullying: Aggressive Behavior and Its Effect on Job Satisfaction and Productivity,* available at www.workplace violence911.com/docs/20081215.pdf.

Dr. Judy is currently researching and writing the topics of bullying and on the emotion of Joy. In addition, she is a Life Coach, coaching leaders on how to develop High Performance Organizations and coaching the targets of workplace bullies. More of her writings on different topics can be found in current and future volumes of *The Refractive Thinker,* available on www.refractivethinker.com. Additional articles about Dr. Judy's work may be found at www.workplaceviolence911.com/ docs/20081215.pdf.

To reach Dr. Judy Fisher-Blando for information on any of these topics, and for executive coaching or coaching on workplace bullying, please e-mail drjudyblando@yahoo.com.

Dr. Thomas G. Robinson, Jr., holds a Bachelor of Science (BS) from James Madison University; a Master of Business Administration (MBA) from National University; and a Doctorate of Management (DM) in Organizational Leadership from the University of Phoenix School of Advanced Studies.

Dr. Robinson is Author, Poet, Artist, Musician, Lecturer, and Technology professional, with over 25 years of progressive leadership experience in directing rapidly changing technologies for The United States Marine Corps, American Telephone & Telegraph Company, Lucent Technologies, and Verizon. He received his Project Management Professional (PMP) certification from the Project Management Institute and his Program Management Masters Certification from George Washington University.

Dr. Robinson is the Co-owner of Perez-Robinson & Sons, LLC a Management Consulting Company specializing in Human Capital Management & Integration (HCM&I) and coaching Executive Leadership.

To reach Dr. Robinson for information on any of these topics, please e-mail: tgrobinson@verizon.net.

Southern Nevadan author **Dr. Cheryl A. Lentz** holds several nationally accredited degrees; a Bachelor of Arts (BA) from the University of Illinois, Urbana-Champaign; a Master of Science in International Relations (MSIR) from Troy University; and a Doctorate of Management (DM) in Organizational Leadership from the University of Phoenix School of Advanced Studies.

Dr. Cheryl, affectionately known as 'Doc C' to her students, is a university professor on faculty with Embry-Riddle University, Colorado State University-Global, The University of the Rockies, and the University of Phoenix where she also serves on several doctoral committees and is a faculty mentor. Dr. Cheryl also offers expertise in editing for APA style for graduate thesis and doctoral dissertations.

Dr. Cheryl is also an active member of Alpha Sigma Alpha Sorority.

Additional published works include her dissertation: *Strategic Decision Making in Organizational Performance: A Quantitative Study of Employee Inclusiveness, The Golden Palace Theory of Management, Journey Outside the Golden Palace, The Refractive Thinker: Vol. I: An Anthology of Doctoral Learners, Vol. II: Research Methodology,* and *Vol. III: Change Management.* For additional details, please visit her website: www.drcheryllentz.com

To reach Dr. Cheryl Lentz for information on any of these topics, and please e-mail: drcheryllentz@gmail.com

CHAPTER 10

Maximizing Debt Collection Performance Through Organizational Design Changes

Dr. Kaja Kroll

As evidenced in the 2008 global financial crisis, achieving superior debt collection performance levels continues to be one of the main challenges of the financial services industry worldwide. In 2007, a significant number of mortgage consumers were delinquent in their monthly debt payments and collection call centers of financial institutions found it difficult to bring the accounts current. Many banks had to register uncollected mortgage loans as losses, which affected the bottom line of the company's financial profit and loss statement (Blundell-Wignall, 2008). The inability to collect outstanding mortgage loans drove the US market towards a recession, negatively affected the banking system around the world, and evolved into a global financial crisis in 2008 (Hornero, 2008). During the global financial crisis, governments throughout the world had to bail out banks to recreate consumer confidence in the market.

Due to the immense impact of uncollected loans on profits, the performance of collection call centers is becoming more critical for the success, sustainability, and viability of financial institutions. Effective collection performance is vital for the overall society (Rippentrop, 2007), because "the more difficult (or costly) it is to ensure that a loan is repaid, the higher will be the costs of borrowing, and less credit will generally be available" (Hunt, 2007, p. 11). In turn, an increase in consumer loans significantly stimulates the economic development of a country through increased customer spending (Bertocco, 2005).

According to the Mexico Bank Association (2008), overall consumer delinquency rates more than doubled from 2005 to 2008 in Mexico (p. 8), and the delinquent debt increased by 450% in the same time-frame (p. 12). The Bank of Mexico further reported that delinquency rates in Mexico are twice as high as in the United States (Becerra, 2008, p. 1). Several researchers claimed that the job design of a call center can significantly influence the performance of Customer Service Representatives (CSRs), but substantial controversy exists about the appropriate work structure (Murray, Jordan, & Bowden, 2004; Sprigg & Jackson, 2006). Most call centers apply the traditional production line approach while others use job design models based on employee involvement theories (Batt, 2002). The present chapter summarizes the results of Kroll's (2009) dissertation that examined the impact of job design on collection performance in a contact center of a major financial services company located in Mexico.

Purpose and Nature of Kroll's Research Study

The purpose of Kroll's (2009) quantitative, quasi-experimental study was to determine any significant differences of two job design models on the impact of collection productivity and effectiveness of 60 part-time and full-time CSRs within a collection contact center of a financial services company operating in Monterrey, Mexico. The company researched works in a non-union environment. The research study advanced knowledge by: (a) understanding cause and effect between job design models and performance, (b) broadening the understanding of collection practices, and (c) expanding on call center industry research in Mexico.

Kroll's (2009) research was conducted in a large financial services company that specializes in automotive financing and is headquartered in the United States. The population related to the study included all CSRs working at the six collection contact centers of the company. The selected sample for the study was the operations center of the organization in Monterrey, Mexico, including 60 part-time and full-time CSRs who work delinquent accounts between 31 and 120 days past due.

In the study, the relational linkages between job design (independent variable) and collection output (dependent variable) were determined. The job design models tested included the Scientific Production Line Model (SPLM) and the Alignment-High Involvement Model (AHIM). Table 1, on the following page, summarizes the comparison and contrast of the two job design models. The SPLM is based on Taylor's (1916) command and control principles and can be described as a "formalized, bureaucratic system" or service factory that aims at achieving maximum productivity" (Pruijt, 2000, p. 446). In contrast, the AHIM follows the principles of participative management, aligns measurement and reward systems with strategic organizational goals, and gives employees the autonomy to deliver results based on individual-level ownership and accountability (Kanter, 1983; Semler, 1997).

The dependent variable was defined as collection performance including collection productivity and collection effectiveness. Both collection productivity and effectiveness are aggregate scores of four specific collection metrics. The productivity metrics comprised the number of collection calls handled per CSR, the number of payment promises made and kept per hour, and the money collected. The effectiveness metrics consisted of two delinquency levels, including accounts with more than 30 days past due and with more than 60 days past due (i.e., the delinquency level is a ratio that calculates the number of accounts that are more than

TABLE 1. COMPARISON AND CONTRAST OF AHIM AND SPLM

	Alignment High-Involvement Model (AHIM)	Scientific Production Line Model (SPLM)
Theoretical framework	Semler's (1997) alignment theory, Kanter's (1983) participative management philosophy	Taylor's (1916) command and control principles, scientific management approach
Results achieved	Employee ownership and discretionary effort	Focus on efficiency in a service factory
Level of CSR autonomy	High CSR empowerment to determine daily collection strategy	Low empowerment of CSRs. Team leaders determine collection strategy
Goal alignment	Individual CSR goals are aligned to strategic organizational goals	Individual CSR goals are not aligned to strategic organizational goals
Primary focus of CSRs	Collection effectiveness (30+ and 60+ delinquency, number and amount of charge-offs)	Collection productivity (number of calls, number of promises made and kept, amount collected)
Role of team leaders	Coach employees to become more effective CSRs	Give clear instructions to CSRs to ensure maximum productivity
Purpose of call monitoring	Coaching tool	Ensure quality compliance

30 and 60 days past due measured against the total portfolio) as well as the number and amount of charged-off accounts (i.e., the volume and monetary value of accounts that are written off as uncollectible loans).

In the research study, only the job design model for the PM

experimental group was changed and all other variables were held constant for both groups. Supervisors, team leaders, and CSRs of the evening shift received special training sessions about the production line method so that they could quickly adapt to the new model. Even though the study accounted for manipulation and control, only a quasi-experiment was feasible. A convenience sample was applied instead of using a random assignment of the participating CSRs to groups. Consequently, in the quasi-experiment causal conclusions between job design and collection performance were limited because no random assignment of participants to the control and experimental groups could be realized. The next section illustrates the research questions and hypotheses of the study.

Research Questions and Hypotheses

Kroll's (2009) quantitative, quasi-experimental research study examined the relational linkages between job design and collection output. The research study was guided by the central question of how job design affects collection performance in a contact center located in Mexico. This question was the focal point of the whole research study and led to the more specific research questions: (a) Does average CSR productivity vary under different job designs? (b) Does average CSR effectiveness vary under different job designs?

Two specific hypotheses were defined based on the research questions.

Hypothesis H_{01} (Null Hypothesis): Average CSR productivity does not show any significant differences under different job designs in a contact center of a financial services company.

Hypothesis H_{02} (Null Hypothesis): Average CSR effectiveness does not show any significant differences under different job designs in a contact center of a financial services company.

Theoretical Framework

Kroll's (2009) quantitative, quasi-experimental research study examined the impact of two job design models on collection performance. The foundation of the job design models was constructed by Smith's (1776) and Fayol's (1916) division of labor, Taylor's (1916) scientific management, Hackman and Oldham's (1980) job redesign, Kanter's (1983) empowerment approach, and Semler's (1997) alignment theory. Chase, Jacobs and Aquilano's (2004) socio-technical systems represented contemporary job design theory. The conceptual framework of performance theory was based on Daniels' (1995) breakthrough performance as well as Kaplan and Norton's (2004) "balanced scorecard" (p. 28) that combined qualitative and quantitative performance measures. The debt collection model of Lawrence and Solom (2002) served was the cornerstone to enhance CSR productivity and effectiveness metrics.

Data Analysis

Collection performance data gathered from the company's reporting system were downloaded to a data file. Demographic data were classified and tabulated, including gender, age range, job tenure, and educational level, for descriptive analysis and reporting. No missing data were identified at the individual level for any of the productivity and effectiveness measures. Individual values, means, and standard deviations for the dependent variable of collection productivity and effectiveness were calculated and presented in tabular format.

To test the hypotheses, Analysis of Variance (ANOVA) was applied to determine if a significant difference in performance existed comparing the baseline and posttest data between the two groups (control versus experimental group). The p value was also determined allowing the researcher to accept or reject the null hypotheses. Descriptive and graphical analysis complemented the ANOVA.

Findings and Interpretations

Hypothesis 1 Testing

The first null hypothesis H_{01} states that average CSR productivity does not significantly vary under different job designs in a contact center of a financial services company (H_{01}: $\mu_1 = \mu_2$). The findings of the first hypothesis testing the relationship of job design and CSR productivity are consistent employing descriptive and graphical analysis as well as ANOVA. The ANOVA determined a significant productivity difference between the AM control group that continued to work under the AHIM work structure and the PM experimental group that was exposed to the SPLM job design, $F(1, 59) =$ 16.36, $p = .0002$ (two-tailed). The null hypothesis was rejected, with $p < .05$ indicating that job design influences CSR productivity.

The significant difference in productivity of the PM experimental group versus the AM control group indicates that the SPLM job design is delivering higher productivity results than the AHIM work design. These findings of increased productivity under the SPLM job design concur with Taylor's (1916) scientific management approach in which specific output requirements are defined and enforced to maximize individual throughput. The findings of the first hypothesis testing also supported the foundational theories of Smith (1776) and Fayol (1916), who proposed a very structured job design using the division of labor and specialization to realize maximum productivity and efficiency gains. Consequently, the foundational theories of Hackman and Oldham (1980), Kanter (1983), and Semler (1997), which favor a job design that gives employees the opportunity to execute the complete task with complete autonomy and ownership to increase CSR performance, were not supported.

The outcome of the descriptive analysis indicated that the SPLM job design generates overall higher productivity results than the AHIM work structure with a performance difference of 211.1%.

The production line approach of the PM group also led to a decrease in the productivity standard deviations whereas the AM group reported similar levels of variance throughout the quasi-experiment. The Collection Manager identified the following three success factors for increasing the productivity of the PM experimental group that worked under the SPLM work design: (a) definition of hourly, weekly, and monthly productivity goals per CSR, (b) close supervision of the team leaders to ensure that hourly productivity goals were met, and (c) CSR consequences for non-compliance (B. Hernandez, personal communication, October 20, 2008).

As a consequence for not delivering the expected work performance in the allotted timeframe, employees of the PM experimental group were encouraged by their team leaders to spend unpaid overtime to make up for the lost productivity. Approximately 10% of the PM CSRs worked some overtime to meet their daily productivity results during the quasi-experiment. The outcome of the first hypothesis concurs with Lawrence and Solomon (2002), who had predicted that the SPLM job design with a production focus leads to higher productivity output because "what you measure is what you get" (p. 167). Townsend (2005) concurred that most call centers are "post-industrial Tayloristic production lines" (p. 47). Several authors attested that the predominant job design in call centers in the world is based on Taylor's (1916) command and control principles to achieve increased productivity (Batt, 2002; Brannan, 2005; Budhwar, et al., 2006; Larsen, 2005; Murray, et al., 2004; Sprigg & Jackson, 2006; Wickham and Collins, 2004). The findings of the first hypothesis, though, are contradictory to Arthur (1994) and Budhwar, et al. (2006), who found that companies using the commitment system (AHIM) realized higher productivity gains and lower turnover in comparison to companies that applied the control system (SPLM).

Kroll's (2009) study was constrained to a 2-month period, which raises the question if the superior productivity results under the

SPLM job design are sustainable over time. Lawrence and Solomon (2002) confirmed that productivity improvements can be realized more quickly by applying a production line focus because CSRs are pressured to fulfill the minimum hourly output requirements. Prujit (2000) and Brödner (2007) argued that the application of a service factory is likely to increase CSR stress, discontentment, and turnover. Batt (2002) also recognized that the traditional production line approach leads to high individual efficiency but also entails low levels of employee satisfaction and loyalty due to the lack of human involvement. Murray, et al. (2004) identified that the absence of employee empowerment in call centers often leads to employee stress, burnout, CSR dissatisfaction, and high levels of attrition. In contrast to the literature review support indicating that a production line job design leads to higher CSR turnover (Batt, Brödner, Murray et al., Prujit), no CSR attrition was recorded in the PM experimental group that was exposed to the SPLM job design. Only 1 CSR of the AM control group left the company for a better job opportunity during the baseline month, which was considered insignificant for the quasi-experiment. The next subsection contains the findings and conclusions of the second hypothesis of Kroll's research study.

Hypothesis 2 Testing

The second null hypothesis H_{02} states that average CSR effectiveness does not significantly vary under different job designs in a contact center of a financial services company (H_{02}: $\mu_1 = \mu_2$). The ANOVA did not show a significant effectiveness difference between the AM control group that continued to work under the AHIM work structure and the PM experimental group that was exposed to the SPLM job design, $F(1, 59) = 1.66$, $p = .2027$ (two-tailed). The null hypothesis was not rejected, with $p > .05$, suggesting that job design does not influence CSR effectiveness. In contrast to the expectation of the company being researched, the PM group that worked under the SPLM job design realized greater, yet statistically insignificant, effectiveness improvements than the AM group that continued to work under the AHIM throughout the quasi-experiment. The outcome of the second hypotheses, testing the relationship of job design on CSR effectiveness, did not support the findings of Hackman and Oldham (1980), Kanter (1983) and Semler (1997) who predicted a significantly superior performance output under the AHIM job design.

The effectiveness difference of 33.7% between the two groups is an indicator that job design could affect CSR effectiveness over time. The length of 2 months for the quasi-experiment could have been insufficient to show significant effectiveness differences in the ANOVA. Lawrence and Solomon (2002) claimed that effectiveness results are lagging indicators of productivity outputs. In collection call centers, the probability of payments increases in relation to the number of customer contacts made (Lawrence & Solomon). In turn, an increase in money collected will naturally reduce loss exposure. The PM experimental group applied a service factory approach to maximize the productivity outcome in order to consequently influence the amount of charge-offs, the most important effectiveness indicator. The PM group collected more money and reported a higher decrease in the amount charged-off in comparison to the AM group. The outcome of the productivity and effectiveness analysis supports the finding of Lawrence and Solomon (2002), who claimed that the productivity outcome is critical to improve collection effectiveness. The next section includes a discussion of the implications and significance of the findings for several stakeholders.

Study Implications

Kroll's (2009) research study provided information of significance for organizations, collection leaders, employees, researchers and theory as well as the government and society overall. The study contributed to closing the gap in knowledge by simultaneously comparing the impact of two job designs (the traditional production line approach and the alignment-high-involvement model) on individual CSR productivity and effectiveness results. Lawrence and Solomon (2002) stated that a small change in collection performance can have a major impact on the profitability of a company. A lending institution with strong collection performance has a strategic advantage over the competition because the company can accept higher-risk customers (Lawrence & Solomon).

The extended collection performance model shown in Figure 1 broadens the debt collection model of Lawrence and Solomon

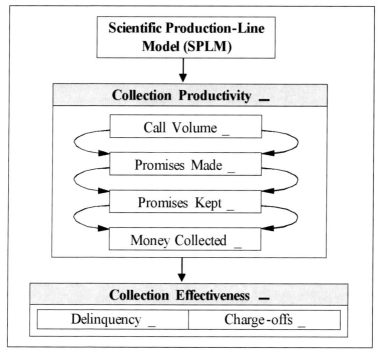

Figure 1: Extended collection performance model.

by integrating the variable of job design. Specifically, the SPLM work structure was added to the model because the first hypothesis, testing the impact of job design on CSR productivity, indicated that the production line approach leads to significantly superior productivity results than the AHIM job design, F (1, 59) = 16.36, p < .05.

The extended model shows that the SPLM job design leads to higher collection productivity results, defined by call volume, the number of promises made and kept, and the amounts collected. Increasing the number of CSR calls per hour enhances the probability of customer contacts and the ability to obtain payment promises from customers. In turn, increasing the number of payment promises per hour raises the likelihood of collecting higher levels of outstanding balances. Consistent with the findings of Lawrence and Solomon (2002), collection productivity then leads to higher collection effectiveness results. The significance of improved productivity is that an increase in the amount collected improves collection effectiveness by lowering delinquency rates and reducing charge-offs. Achieving lower credit losses is the ultimate goal of the collection department. The study findings revealed that the SPLM job design leads to increased, yet statistically insignificant, collection effectiveness results, $F(1, 59) = 1.66, p > .05$.

Recommendations for Future Action

Based on the research findings and the extended collection performance model, several recommendations can be made. As confirmed by the first hypothesis, testing the impact of job design on CSR productivity, managers of collection departments should use the SPLM job design if the main goal is to increase CSR productivity. Using a service factory approach in collections allows leaders to take control over the collection output and ensure short-term results in terms of call volume, payment promises taken and kept, and amounts collected. The long-term sustainability of the production line approach though has to be verified because several authors raised the concern of increased CSR attrition over time (Batt, 2002; Murray, et al., 2004; Whitt, 2006). Although no turnover was registered in the PM group during the 2-month quasi-experiment, superior performance results of the SPLM job design versus the AHIM job design should be validated by a longitudinal study of at least 6 months. Business consultants can also recommend the SPLM job design to increase productivity in collection contact centers. However, a significant difference in effectiveness results between the AHIM and SPLM job designs was not found, $F(1, 59) = 1.66$, $p > .05$.

Financial institutions and businesses with collection activities should pay more attention to collection performance. As reflected in the 2008 global financial crisis, a company can only survive if outstanding loans are collected. In turn, financial institutions will prosper and offer more financing options if the debt collection operation is performing at high levels of CSR productivity and effectiveness.

Society in general may be able to benefit from the results of Kroll's (2009) study should the recommendation be implemented to apply the SPLM job design in collection contact centers. An increase in collection performance will raise the level of success and cash flow, which, in turn, would allow financial institutions to offer more loans that would have the effect of stimulating consumer spending and economic growth (Hunt, 2007). The inability to collect outstanding loans can even lead to a financial crisis, with a substantial reduction of credit lines and the increase of interest rates as demonstrated in the 2008 global financial crisis. In turn, effective collection performance would increase the availability of consumer loans and would stimulate again the economic development of a country through increased customer spending (Bertocco, 2005). Governments and policy makers should also reinforce the need for companies to establish effective collection operations before expanding their credit lines to prevent future global financial crisis. In the next section, several suggestions for future research are formulated to minimize the study limitations.

Limitations and Suggestions for Future Research

Kroll's (2009) study was conducted as a 2-month quasi-experiment. The limited time frame could have been insufficient to test the sustainability of the superior productivity outcome and determine any significant effectiveness results under the SPLM job design. Increasing the length of the quasi-experiment for at least six months is recommended to determine if significant differences exist in CSR effectiveness of both groups.

To accept or reject the hypotheses of the research study, the productivity and effectiveness indicators were combined into aggregate scores with percentage weights of the researched company. Future research should determine the impact of job designs on each performance indicator separately. Furthermore, the measurement of additional performance indicators could complement the findings of the research study, such as customer satisfaction measures to evaluate the service perception of customers as well as cure and roll percentages to determine the number of accounts moving between delinquency stages.

To improve the generalization of Kroll's (2009) study, future research should expand the data collected beyond a single firm, industry, and geographic location. As this research focused on the 31 to 120 days past due delinquency range, the study design should also be replicated using CSRs who collect in different delinquency stages. The applicability of the findings of Kroll's research study should be tested with other financing options like credit cards or mortgage loans because the study focused on only automotive financing. Additionally, the study analyzed the impact of job designs on debt collection performance. Subsequent research may attempt to replicate the study using call centers with alternate purposes such as, customer service, sales, and helpdesk operations.

The interpretation of the findings of the hypotheses testing were limited because of the size of the entire collection department consisted of only 60 CSRs. Future research should use a large enough sample size to apply advanced statistical procedures. Results would approximate a normal distribution with lower levels of variance. Future research should also consider the application of a true experiment with random assignment to improve the examination of the causality between job design and collection performance.

A methodological suggestion for future research includes interviews and focus groups of key participants. The use of mixed methods research could help explore deeper insights from CSRs and management relative to their attitudes towards the two job designs and the applied leadership behaviors of the supervisor team. Furthermore, future research may consider the use of correlational analysis of the individual performance metrics to assess the consistency of the extended collection performance model. Apart from collection performance implications, future research may further explore the merits and demerits of the SPLM and AHIM job designs in general.

Several authors stated that neither the traditional production line approach nor the alignment and high-involvement approaches are optimal job designs for call centers (Budhwar, et al., 2006; Frenkel, et al., 1998; Murray, et al., 2004; Ojha & Kasturi, 2005; Townsend, 2005). Using a hybrid model between Taylorism and high-involvement job designs might minimize the disadvantages of these extreme work structures. Consequently, research should be conducted that investigates the impact of AHIM, SPLM, and hybrid job design interventions simultaneously.

CONCLUSIONS

The present chapter summarized Kroll's (2009) quantitative, quasi-experimental study that determined any significant differences in the impact of two job design models on collection performance at a collection contact center of a major financial services company in Mexico. The job design models tested in the study included the SPLM based on Taylor's (1916) command and control principles as well as the AHIM based on Kanter's (1983) employee involvement approach and Semler's (1997) alignment theory. Collection performance in the study consisted of both productivity and effectiveness metrics. The PM experimental group with the SPLM job design showed a significantly greater improvement of the aggregate productivity results when compared to the AM control group that continued to work under the AHIM structure with a performance difference of 211.1%. The result of the second hypothesis did not support that job design has a significant impact on collection effectiveness. The statistical analysis though indicated a slightly greater effectiveness improvement of the PM experimental group that worked under the SPLM job design with a performance difference of 33.7% in comparison to the AM control group. Based on the study findings, Kroll presented a debt collection model that applied the SPLM job design to enhance both collection productivity and effectiveness. Financial institutions should implement the SPLM job design in their debt collection centers to mitigate the impact of the global financial crisis. Improved debt collection performance should increase the availability of consumer loans and stimulate the economic development worldwide.

References

Arthur, J. B. (1994). Effects of human resource systems on manufacturing performance and turnover. *Academy of Management Journal, 38*(1), 670–687.

Batt, R. (2002, June). Managing customer services: Human resource practices, quit rates, and sales growth. *Academy of Management Journal, 45*(3), 587–597. Retrieved from EbscoHost database.

Becerra, J. (2008, August 22). Mexico doubles delinquency levels. *Reforma,* Business Section, p. 1.

Bertocco, G. (2005, October). The role of credit in a Keynesian monetary economy. *Review of Political Economy, 17*(4), 489–511. Retrieved from EbscoHost database.

Blundell-Wignall, A. (2008). The subprime crisis: Size, deleveraging and some policy options. *OECD Journal, 1*(1) 29–53. Retrieved from EbscoHost database.

Brannan, M. J. (2005, September). Once more with feeling: Ethnographic reflections on the mediation of tension in a small team of call centre workers. *Work & Organization, 12*(5), 420–439. Retrieved August 26, 2007, from EbscoHost database.

Brödner, P. (2007, June). From Taylorism to competence-based production. *AI & Society, 21*(4), 497–515. Retrieved from ProQuest database.

Budhwar, P., Varma, A., Singh, V., & Dhar, R. (2006, May). HRM systems of Indian call centres: An exploratory study. *International Journal of Human Resource Management, 17*(5), 881–897. Retrieved from EbscoHost database.

Chase, R. B., Jacobs, F. R., & Aquilano, N. J. (2004). *Operations management for competitive advantage* (10th ed.). New-York: McGraw-Hill.

Daniels, W. (1995). *Breakthrough performance.* Mill Valley. CA: Act Publishing.

Fayol, H. (1916). *General and industrial management.* London: Pitman Publishing.

Frenkel, S. J., Tam, M., Korcynski, M., & Shire, K. (1998). Beyond bueaurocracy?—Work

Hackman J. R., & Oldham, S. (1980). *Work redesign.* Reading. MA: Addison Wesley.

Hornero, A. C. (2008). The crisis of suprime loans and the risk of a credit crunch. *Journal* of Global Economics. Retrieved from EbscoHost database.

Hunt, R. M. (2007). Collecting consumer debt in America. *Business Review* (Federal Reserve Bank of Philadelphia, p. 11–24). Retrieved from EbscoHost database.

Kanter, R. M. (1983). Dilemmas of Managing Participation. *Organizational Dynamics, 11*(1), 5–27. Retrieved from EbscoHost database.

Kaplan, R. S., & Norton, D. P. (2004). *Strategy maps: Converting intangible assets into tangible outcomes.* Harvard: Harvard Business School Press.

Kroll, K. (2009, August). *The impact of job design on debt collection performance in a Mexican contact center.*

Larsen, A. C. (2005, June). In the public interest: autonomy and resistance to methods of standardising nurses' advice and practices from a health call centre in Perth, Western Australia. *Nursing Inquiry, 12*(2), 135–143. Retrieved from EbscoHost database.

Lawrence, D., & Solomon, A. (2002). *Managing a consumer lending business.* New York: Solomon and Lawrence Partners.

Mexico Bank Association (2008, October). *Mexico banking industry report for October.*

Murray, J., Jordan, P., & Bowden, B. (2004, October). An empirical study of job design in the Australian call centre industry. *International Journal of Employment Studies, 12*(2), 3–26. Retrieved August 26, 2007; from EbscoHost database.

Ojha, A. K., & Kasturi, A. (2005, March). 'Successful' call centre employees: Understanding employee attributes and performance evaluation processes. *New Technology, Work & Employment, 20*(1), 47–59. Retrieved from EbscoHost database.

Pruijt, H. (2000). Repainting, modifying, smashing Taylorism. *Journal of Organizational Change Management, 13*(5) 13. Retrieved from EbscoHost database.

Rippentrop, G. (2007, November). *Debt collection by the numbers. Sizing up the Industry.* Paper presented at the First World Credit and Collections Congress, Mexico-City, Mexico.

Semler, S. W. (1997). Systematic agreement: A theory of organizational alignment. *Human Resource Development Quarterly, 8,* 23–40.

Smith, A. (1776). *The wealth of nations.* New York: Modern Library.

Sprigg, C., & Jackson, P. R. (2006, April). Call centers as lean service environments: Job-related strain and the mediating role of work design. *Journal of Occupational Health Psychology, 11*(2), 197–212. Retrieved from EbscoHost database.

Taylor, F. W. (1916). The principles of scientific management. *Bulletin of the Taylor Society.*

Townsend, K. (2005, March). Electronic surveillance and cohesive teams: room for resistance in an Australian call centre? *New Technology, Work & Employment, 20*(1), 47–59. Retrieved from EbscoHost database.

Whitt, W. (2006). The impact of increased employee retention on performance in a customer contact center. *Manufacturing and Service Operations Management, 8*(3), 235–252. Retrieved from EbscoHost database.

Wickham, J., & Collins, G. (2004, January). The call centre: A nursery for new forms of work organisation? *Service Industries Journal, 24*(1), 1–18. Retrieved from EbscoHost database.

About the Author

Dr. Kaja Kroll holds several business degrees; a Bachelor in Business Administration (BA) from Berufsakademie, Berlin, Germany; a Global MBA from Thunderbird School of Global Management, US and the Instituto Technológico y de Estudios Superiores de Monterrey (ITESM), Mexico; a Magister and Master Coach certification from The International School of Coaching, Spain; and a Doctorate of Management in Organizational Leadership (DM) from University of Phoenix School of Advanced Studies, US.

Dr. Kroll has been working in senior management and executive positions in the financial services industry in several countries. She works as MBA professor with the Escuela de Graduados en Administración y Dirección de Empresas (EGADE), Mexico; and teaches the strategic debt collection management specialization for the University Anahuac, Mexico. Dr. Kroll also offers her expertise as an organizational development consultant and participates as speaker and panelist at global customer service and debt collection conferences.

Additional published works include her dissertation: *The Impact of Job Design on Debt Collection Performance in a Mexican Contact Center.*

To reach Dr. Kaja Kroll for information on any of these topics, please e-mail: kaja.kroll@gmail.com.

CHAPTER 11

Systems Theory: Changing the Hegemonic Impact on Leadership Advancement for Women

Dr. Beverly D. Carter

Organizations are comprised of individuals who are composites of their mental models. These models include culture, gender, thinking styles, leadership styles or multiple intelligences which will be discussed further (see Figure 1). In the current economic crisis, organizations are challenged to survive in turbulent times. These economic times have been defined by Ponzi schemes that shook the core of our global, financial structure, characterized by dishonesty in business.

What happens when there is inequality and bias within the ranks of an organization? Systems Theory provides a unique window into the psyche of an organization's mental models. Decision-making that parallels the values of society, and the way in which resources are allocated in society, are ordinarily determined by people in positions of power. Understanding mental models of prejudice, bias, and subordination associated with the roles of women and the outcome of these associations is vital to understanding the limited access of women to powerful leadership positions.

Gardner's (1983/2004) *theory of multiple intelligences* suggests that people use a large number of abilities in order to synthesize their experiences of the world. These abilities are based on several categories of mental models that advocate a certain type of information. The identified mental models are linguistic, mathematical/logical,

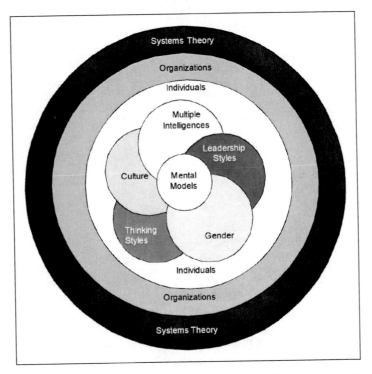

Figure 1. Diagram of mental models of leadership advancement for women.

musical /rhythmic, bodily/kinesthetic, visual/spatial, personal/emotional and existential. Gardner (1989) posited that by limiting our categories of perception, information processing, and problem solving to a narrow range of abilities, theories are created that offer a greater propensity of being biased.

According to Harquail (2002), the basic premise of the multiple intelligences typology was found in the ability of people within organizations to process information that included, but was not limited to, verbal and logical capacities. "The six types of mental models are quasi-independent and correlated, because they are different manifestations of the same organization" (Harquail, p. 2).

Mental models were determined to be significant when relating to an organization's identified leadership and barriers to women's advancement within these organizations. The premise behind mental models in the leadership advancement of women, based upon the poor representation of women in executive leadership positions, is twofold. First, there is a greater propensity toward prejudice and bias toward women that continue to perpetuate the problem and act as barriers to the advancement of women via a masculine group-think concept. Second, by limiting the interaction with women at executive leadership levels, organizations will not benefit from the female decision-making perspective, which represents a large portion of the American and world public.

GENDER AND ORGANIZATIONAL LEADERSHIP

Schein began researching sex-role stereotyping in leadership advancement and management characteristics in the United States almost 30 years ago. Since that time, numerous replications of Schein's study have taken place in the United States and in the international community. The main issue uncovered in these studies supports the theory that managerial sex typing is a major psychological barrier to the advancement of women in the United States.

Globalization has expanded this issue to the international arena by highlighting the fact that women in management are faced with barriers to leadership advancement world-wide (Schein, 2001). Compared to men, women do not have equal access to power and organizational leadership positions. According to former President Clinton, "the tops of managerial and governmental hierarchies do not look like America" (Carli & Eagly, 2001, p. 3). Sellers, as cited in Dennis and Kunkel (2004), postulated that at the turn of the 20th century, only six women held CEO positions in Fortune 500 companies.

Schein (2001) stated that managerial sex typing has created a serious psychological barrier to the advancement of women in America. Gender-related stereotypes and the expectations of and for women based upon stereotypes ensure that organizations must revisit cultural mental models to create equal opportunities for women who aspire to senior positions. The United States, the most advanced industrial society, is still moving very slowly toward gender equality. In fact, over the past decade, the presence of a very small number of women in leadership positions supports the existence of the glass ceiling metaphor. The glass ceiling metaphor represents an unseen barrier that is powerful enough to prevent women from advancing beyond a certain level (Carli & Eagly, 2001).

Many organizational leaders in Western society represent businesses aligned with the acceptance of masculinity as the defining characteristic of leadership. As a result, women have been kept out of leadership because organizational leadership, through its emphasis on masculinity, confirms men's power and control (Theberge, 1987). The assumed helplessness of women and other subordinate groups is therefore considered a normal reality or commonsense. Hegemony as a concept relates to social institutions and organizations that are maintained through reproduction in society. It is also espoused as a norm in cultural institutions and perpetuated through the mass media. This effect seems to "naturalize men's power and privilege over women" (Whisenant, Pedersen, & Obenour, 2002, p. 486).

Numerous barriers assist in the promulgation of the glass ceiling, or the hegemonic reality faced by many women in business. Women are not perceived as tough enough for line jobs but seen as being expressive or communal, with a disposition to being sensitive and nurturing, and therefore nudged into the areas of human resources or public relations (Haslett, Geis, & Carter, 1992). Line officer jobs, however, involve financial management, an area where women are not well represented, and often lead to promotions to executive leadership. Davison and Burke (2000) in a study of employee selection also found that mental models colored the decision-making process, perceptions, and judgments of decision-makers. According to Heilman (2001), the expectation of a negative performance contributed to the gender-specific manner in which women were depicted.

Coakley (2001) reported that one of the reasons women were underrepresented in major decision-making positions was because of a lack of networking opportunities available to women as compared to their male counterparts. Men essentially had more strategic professional associations in business. According to Hovden (2000), many women appeared less qualified in the subjective evaluation of different job searches as compared to men. Additional barriers are presented by several organizational cultures that are not readily diverse and open to varied viewpoints.

Haben (2001) said it is important to realize the full potential of everyone in the work force to produce better business results, thus giving the process its own momentum. However, according to Schein (2001), women consider male stereotyping as the major barrier—again, gender stereotyping, suggesting that women lack the masculine characteristics required for tough line positions. The insidious effects of these stereotypes can be devastating to career women. Schein (2001) further postulates that such male decision-making attitudes of sex typing management positions seem to go unchecked.

Hegemonic masculinity is deeply entrenched among the more powerful leadership positions of many American organizations. Schein (1985) indicates that "organizations tend to find attractive those candidates who resemble present members in style, assumptions, values, and beliefs" (p. 235). The issues perpetuated by this concept create barriers to the advancement of women to senior leadership positions. Unless there are changes made within the culture of organizations, gender equality will not happen and substantial numbers of women will not advance to executive leadership positions. Systems Theory offers possible solutions to the barriers to leadership advancement opportunities for women and other minorities. Many scholars suggest that women should challenge the status quo that supports hegemonic masculinity found in top leadership positions instead of trying to adopt the male characteristics of executive leaders (Burrell, 1984; Hearn & Parkin, 1983; Mills & Tancred, 1992).

Systems Theory

The following section serves as a view of systems theory as presented by Capra (1996), Checkland (1999), Senge (1990), and Gardner (1993). A synthesis and explanation of the properties of organisms and social systems are reviewed. Ecosystems are also reviewed in their various stages of wholeness as they may provide insight into mental models.

There are three different levels of systems theory as presented in Capra (1996): basic or general system science, complexity/chaos, and quantum systems theory. A look at the application of systems theory and systems thinking from the perspective offered by Checkland (1999) through his work with hard and soft systems are important to the development of this section. Senge's (1990) five disciplines are also reviewed here in an effort to identify the mental models of social systems within organizations. Gardner (1993) reviews systems theory from the contextualized view of intelligence in the basic framework of his Theory of Multiple Intelligences.

Systems theory offers individuals a tool with which to see the interdependence in the concept of wholeness. Western civilization has utilized the methods of science to identify observations of the world through the use of reductionism, repeatability, and refutation in order to acquire well-tested knowledge of the noted regularities found within the universe (Capra, 1996). Understanding an organization using a systems perspective identifies that each part of the organization is dependent upon the other in the creation of the whole of the organization.

General Systems Science

Ludwig von Bertalanffy has been credited by scientists with the establishment of open systems and general systems theory. Bertalanffy, as cited in Hatch (1997), "presented a theory intended to explain all scientific phenomena across both natural and social sciences from the atom to the molecule, through the single cell, organ and organism up to the level of individuals, groups and societies" (p. 34). Hatch states that Bertalanffy acknowledged that these phenomena were all interrelated because "societies contain groups, groups contain individuals, individuals are comprised of organs, organs of cells, cells of molecules and molecules of atoms" (Hatch, p. 34). Bertalanffy called these groups 'systems' because they are all things that contain interrelated parts. What this means is that a whole system, such as an organization, must be considered in its entirety because it cannot be fully understood by simply analyzing its individual parts. In other words, to truly understand an organizational system, one has to be willing to transcend the individual parts to view the entire system at "its own level of complexity" (Hatch, p. 35).

Complexity

According to Capra (1996), living systems are self-organizing networks with individual parts that are all interconnected and interdependent, which accomplishment is understood by using new mathematical tools that permit scientists to model "the non linear interconnected characteristic of networks" (p. 112). A new discovery, it was referred to as the mathematics of complexity and is technically referred to as dynamical systems theory. The system is more qualitative than quantitative, embodying the shift of emphasis characteristic of systems thinking, "from objects to relationships, quantity to quality and from substance to pattern" (Capra, p. 113).

Chaos

Capra (1996) stated that "the behavior of chaotic systems is not merely random but shows a deeper level of patterned order" (p. 123). Chaotic systems as a patterned order whose distinct shapes and underlying patterns are made visible with the new dynamical systems theory show that there is an order to chaos.

Quantum

Quantum physics relates to atoms and subatomic particles. What it shows is that there are no parts, only patterns, in an inseparable web of relationships. This allows for theory to shift, not only from the parts to the whole, but from objects to relationships. The systems view of objects is identified as a network of relationships inextricable from larger networks, which means that the concept of relationships for a systems thinker is primary and "the boundaries of the discernible patterns (objects) are secondary" (Capra, 1996, p. 37).

According to Checkland (1999), Western civilization has used reductionism, repeatability, and refutation as tools to acquire knowledge in order to identify observations of the world. System science begins with the premise and the antecedents that are related to systems thinking as well as the concepts that compliment classical natural science. These concepts attempt to use a particular set of ideas and systems (a set of elements together which form a whole) to understand the complexity of the world.

There are limitations found in science in that complexity, in general, and social phenomena, in particular, both make problems for science, which science has not been able to deal with the so called "real-world problems" (Checkland, 1999, p. 13). Paradigm shifts in management science, for example, remain essential to the resolution of identified problems in organizations requiring alternatives to management issues. "The systems paradigm is concerned with wholes and their properties as well as their hierarchical arrangement" (Checkland, 1999, p. 13). Systems thinking therefore imply thinking about the world outside of ourselves and how we are connected to that world by utilizing the very concepts or mental models offered by systems science with both hard and soft systems.

Hard Systems

Hard systems thinking is a methodology borrowed from the discipline of engineering. It provides a systems analysis, which is an integral part of providing possibilities via the analysis of different accounts or possible problems. This allows the leader of an organization or project to make an informed choice or decision taking all of the possibilities into account. "The belief that real-world problems can be formulated in this way is the distinguishing characteristic of all hard systems thinking" (Checkland, 1999, p. 15). Hard systems thinking is goal-directed because it begins by defining the desired output or goal to be reached.

According to Checkland (1999), scientists ask if we have learned anything while engineers want to know if it works. This is because the field of science implies that the highest value is given to the advancement of knowledge. The fields of engineering and technology prize highly the successful achievement of the defined purpose. Science assists humanity with the understanding and knowledge of the world and how we are a part of it. The methodology of science, according to Checkland (1999), is to utilize reductionist and repeatable experiments in order to test hypotheses of destruction. This scientific methodology has been used to establish public knowledge, which is disseminated through man-made technology.

Soft Systems

Soft problems relate to the social systems of human activity. Soft systems were derived from the application of the hard system methodology, which was not applicable to soft system problems or social systems with obscure goals. Soft systems allow for entirely unexpected answers to emerge. They are derived from studies begun with the identification of the system and its objectives as they pertain to people in real world situations. The soft system methodology "can thus be seen as a general problem-solving approach appropriate to human activity systems when problems cannot be stated clearly and unambiguously" (Checkland, 1999, p. 191). Soft systems create the parameters for paradigm shifts by exploring ambiguity utilizing systems analysis as a means of allowing for the unexpected answer to emerge.

In order to implement changes that are desirable and feasible, Checkland (1999) describes three types of changes that are possible within organizations. The changes are in structure, in procedure, and in attitude. Structural and procedural changes are relatively simple short-term changes. They may be implemented in organizational groupings through organizational reporting structures or through an organization's structure of functional responsibility under the direction of an organization's leadership. However, changes in attitude warrant a genuine look at the individual and collective consciousness of groups as they relate to expectations regarding appropriate behavior. Changes in attitude also merit viewing roles in an appreciative inquiry mode, which is inclusive of changes in influence. Checkland recommended that monitoring changes in this last area could help to identify any perceived problems and mode for improvement. The implementation of new systems would allow for a more flexible and functional organization relative to the creation of continued trust, understanding, and better programming. A combination of both hard and soft systems could bring notably desired changes to fruition for an organization in the process of becoming a learning organization.

Senge's Five Disciplines

According to Senge (1990), "systems thinking is a conceptual framework, a body of knowledge and tools that have been developed over the past fifty years, to make the full patterns clearer, and to help us to see how to change them effectively" (p. 7). Senge presented systems thinking from the human perspective of the up and coming learning organization. He notes that business and human systems are interconnected by an unseen fabric of interrelated actions as wholes among wholes as opposed to wholes made up of individual parts. Apparently, these actions are not always immediate and can often take years to fully play out their effects on each other.

Senge (1990) described the first principles of systems thinking at a level of direct experience. The universe, world, and humanity are all examples of an *indivisible whole.* Humanity has created boundaries, through its mental models that were both fundamental and arbitrary, thus trapping humanity with its own limitations. Senge's following five disciplines work toward a synthesis of personal accounting and organizational growth. This is an integral part of the journey to becoming conscious within the interconnected whole, a never-ending journey of creation for a learning organization.

Personal Mastery

According to Senge (1990), personal mastery is the learning organization's spiritual foundation because it starts by clarifying the things that are of the utmost importance to individuals. Personal mastery is reflected by the manner in which individuals use their lives for the service of the greatest good. Mastery represents the personal and consistent realization of ideals that are of essential importance to individuals. Organizations are challenged to grow by assisting employees in mastering the desire for personal growth.

Mental Models

Senge (1990) states that mental models are assumptions, generalizations, or pictures of images that are deeply ingrained in the human mind influencing how the world is understood and how action is taken. Often humanity is not aware of the effect that mental models have on human behavior. Within organizational management settings, new ideas and insights into outmoded practices are often in conflict with the organization's powerful, tacit mental models. The discipline of working with mental models begins with learning how to uncover our internal pictures of the world in order to discuss them in a learning environment (Senge).

Shared Vision

Shared vision refers to the ability of an organization's leadership to inspire as well as bring its members together with a common identity and sense of destiny (Senge, 1990). It is incumbent upon leaders to find pictures of the future that foster genuine dedication and participation, but not compliance. If there is a genuine vision, and not the usual "vision statement," people could excel and learn. However, often leaders have personal visions that do not get translated into "shared visions" to galvanize an organization (Senge).

From an organizational perspective, allowing staff to participate in the decision-making is viable. However, quite often it is an ignored resource. An organizational commitment to continued learning and enhancement of an organization's shared vision is essential in the new learning organization (Senge, 1990).

Team Learning

Team learning is a discipline that happens with a group whose combined intelligence often exceeds the individual level of intelligence within the team and where teams, on the other hand, develop an extraordinary capacity for coordinated action (Senge, 1990). A team that is truly learning is capable of achieving truly extraordinary results. The individual members of a team continue to grow more rapidly together than had they not been a part of the group (Senge). Team learning in the postmodern organization is vital because teams, not individuals, are the fundamental learning unit upon which individuals base their mental models.

According to Senge (1990), systems thinking is the fifth discipline. Systems thinking is the discipline that allows for the integration of all of the above principles or disciplines. Together they form an interrelated pattern with powerful results for the learning organization. Each of the individual disciplines is assisted by the other via the concept of systems theory that identifies how the whole can exceed the sum of its individual parts.

Systems thinking can assist individuals in understanding the ways in which organizations view themselves in relation to the world they serve. Many individuals within organizations perceive themselves as independent agents. Many organizational issues are not addressed from the perspective of how personal thoughts and actions create current experiences. "A learning organization is a place where people are continually discovering how they create their reality and how they can change it" (Senge, 1990, p. 13).

The Indivisible Whole

Systems thinking allows individuals to see, experience, and understand the whole picture without boundaries and divisions. The indivisible whole represents the inter/intra connection of the world without boundaries and separations. It recognizes the fact that in reality there are no real separations between people and things, that humanity is interconnected in a myriad of ways. This is the way of systems theory—to see the totality in the concept of wholeness in as much as humans can see where the connection to the web of life begins or ends (Senge, 1990).

The integration of all of the parts of an organization, from personal mastery to team learning, the synergy that is systems thinking or, the fifth discipline, is created. As human systems continue to improve both personal and group skills, learning can be perpetuated by recognizing the importance of the indivisible whole of the organization.

Systems theory offers a contextualized view of intelligence as postulated by Gardner (1993) because it takes into account that human beings are both biological and cultural in nature.

> Even before birth, the immature organism lies in the womb of a woman who has habits, styles, and practices that reflect her culture and subculture. And while it is possible to exaggerate the influence of these prenatal influences, there is no question that the life of the infant after birth is inextricably bound with the practices and assumptions of her culture. (Gardner, p. 220)

All of these views are critical to the understanding of mental models within organizations and the way in which they are formed and affect the decision-making process regarding the selection and promotion of future leaders. These views highlight the idea that cognitive mapping within an organizational culture is based upon the mental models of the established leadership that permeate the entire organization (see Figure 1).

Although Capra (1996), Checkland (1999), Senge (1990), and Gardner (1993) take different approaches to systems thinking, they all seem to have the same basic common denominator with regard to systems, which is that all parts of the whole are interrelated. Such an understanding is essential to the development of future leadership of organizations.

According to Haben (2001), it is just as important to recognize that maximizing opportunity and advancement for women is a fundamental business issue as is productivity, quality, or product development. The global devaluation of women is reflected in the status of women worldwide. Rhoodie (cited in Schein, 2001) states that when comparing the sexes, the social, economic, and political status of women is still one of subordination. The status of women and issues of inequality are deeply ingrained in the cultures, practices, and traditional views of people in the U.S. and around the world. The opportunity to link women with management in order to broaden and enhance the opportunities for women regarding freedom and civil rights may create the changes necessary to realize equality in the work place.

Senge's (1990) five disciplines of the new learning organization are: personal mastery, mental models, systems thinking, building a shared vision among members of an organization, and team learning. The purpose of the five pillars is to assist in the enhancement of organizational leadership skills. Team experiences within organizations that include shared mental models, vision, and personal goals provide valuable tools that can help to create healthier learning organizations that are better able to meet global dictates.

In the case of the organization, which is a microcosm of society, it may be possible that the system can be enhanced by the very nature of a global sense of community. Systems theory suggests the process of reconnecting to the 'web of life' by building and nurturing communities that are sustainable, where people can satisfy needs and aspirations without hurting future generations. It is the way that individuals and organizations can engage to maintain a sustainable future (Capra, 1996).

Organizations are challenged to become learning organizations that will realize the full potential of everyone in the workforce to produce better business results, and challenge the status quo thus giving the process its own momentum. Haben (2001) states, "The closer we come to true equality—the more we release all that untapped potential—the more successful all of our organizations will be" (p. 9).

References

Burrell, G. (1984). Sex and organizational analysis. *Organizational Studies, 5,* 97–118.

Capra, F. (1996). *The web of life: A new scientific understanding of living systems.* New York: Anchor Books.

Carli, L. L., & Eagly, A. H. (2001). Gender, hierarchy, and leadership: An introduction. *Journal of Social Issues, 57*(4), 629.

Checkland, P. (1999). *Systems thinking, systems practice.* New York: John Wiley.

Coakley, J. (2001). *Sport in society: Issues and controversies* (7th ed.). Boston: McGraw Hill.

Davison, H. K., & Burke, M. J. (2000). Sex discrimination in simulated employment contexts: A meta-analytic investigation. *Journal of Vocational Behavior, 56,* 225–248.

Dennis, R. M., & Kunkel, A. D. (2004). Perceptions of men, women, and CEOS: The effects of gender identity. *Social Behavior and Personality, 32*(2), 155–172.

Gardner, H. (1983/2004). *Frames of mind: The theory of multiple intelligences* (20th-anniversary edition). New York: Basic Books.

Gardner, H. (1989). *To open minds.* New York: Basic Books.

Gardner, H. (1993). *Multiple Intelligences: the theory in practice, a reader.* New York: Basic Books.

Haben, M. K. (2001). Shattering the glass ceiling. *Executive Speeches, 15*(5), 4–11.

Harquail, C. V. (2002). We know more than we say: A typology for understanding a manifold organizational identity. *Business Source Premier, 141.*

Haslett, B., Geis, F. L., & Carter, M. R. (1992). *The organizational woman: Power and paradox.* New Jersey: Ablex Publishing Corporation.

Hatch, M. J. (1997). *Organization theory: Modern symbolic and postmodern perspectives.* New York: Oxford University Press.

Hearn, J., & Parkin, P. W. (1983). Gender and organizations: A selective review and a critique of a neglected area. *Organization Studies, 4*(2), 19–242.

Heilman, M. E. (2001). Description and prescription: How gender stereotypes prevent women's ascent up the organizational ladder. *Journal of Social Issues, 57*(4), 657.

Hovden, J. (2000). Gender and leadership selection process in Norwegian sporting organizations. *International Review for the Sociology of Sport. 35,* 75–82.

Mills, A. J. & Tancred, P. (1992). *Gendering organizational analysis.* London: Sage.

Schein, E. H. (1985). *Organizational culture and leadership* (2nd ed.). California: Jossey-Bass.

Schein, V. E. (2001). A global look at psychological barriers to women's progress in management. *Journal of Social Issues, 57,* 675–688.

Senge, P. (1990). *The fifth discipline: The art of the learning organization.* New York: Doubleday.

Theberge, N. (1987). Sport and women's empowerment. *Women's Studies International Forum, 10,* 387–393.

Whisenant, W. A., Pedersen, P. M., & Obenour, B. L. (2002). Success and gender: Determining the rate of advancement for intercollegiate athletic directors. *Sex Roles, 47*(9/10), 485.

About the Author

New York author Dr. Beverly D. Carter holds several nationally accredited degrees; a Bachelor of Arts (BA) in Psychology from Western New England College; a Master of Science (MS) in Adult Education Human Resources Management from Fordham University; and a Doctorate of Management (DM) in Organizational Leadership from the University of Phoenix School of Advanced Studies.

Dr. Carter, is a (1) "corporate physician" with Business Prosperity Solutions where she serves organizations as a mentor and guide as they shift their organizational paradigms, (2) Civil Servant dedicated to program development of subcontracted, not for profit agencies, and (3) volunteer consultant with Ejayes Charities which supports plans for medical missions to serve the underprivileged in Africa and most recently, Haiti.

Dr. Carter won the 2009 Gold NACO award for exceptional development of a county government program for the development of a Roll Call Training for Law Enforcement as "first responders" to caregivers and the growing older driving community.

Additional published works include her dissertation: *The Impact of Thinking and Leadership Styles on the Advancement of Women and a County Government Publication: A Guide for Caregivers* for which she won the 2009 Bronze Achievement Award.

To reach Dr. Beverly Carter for information on any of these topics, and please e-mail: dr.beverlycarter@yahoo.com.

Ethical Leadership Is Part of Globalization

Dr. Thomas M. Woodruff

Volume IV of the Refractive Thinker™ was devoted to ethics, leadership, and globalization. Leadership topics incorporated in this volume included ethical education and decision-making; leadership style and ethical communication; behavior integrity; the ethical responsibility of IT professionals; the importance of the leader's ethical character to the organizational culture; leadership characteristics and communication on social networks; body language; maximizing organizational performance through design changes; and leadership advancement for women. The following is a brief review of these valuable contributions.

Dr. Neysa established the academic tone of this volume by positing that educational leaders should possess a solid foundation in ethical studies to facilitate sound moral decision-making in the many issues that are faced in today's society. To illustrate her premise, Dr. Neysa presented a concise review of ethical philosophies followed by the established theories for developing personal ethical beliefs. She explored ethical decision-making in the subsequent section and concluded with recommendations for educational leaders in general and specifically regarding inclusion, a contemporary ethics issue.

In Chapter 2, Dr. Sheila cited the unethical behavior of leaders in all realms of our global society. She posited that there was a positive correlation between leadership style and communication, and employee and organizational performance. The results of her study confirmed this relationship and concluded the need for leaders to model ethical communication, integrity, and attentiveness to affect organizational performance.

With the foundation for ethical leadership defined in the first two chapters, Dr. Karleen tackled the sensitive issue of physician behavior and communication in addressing end of life treatment options. In this well-written presentation, the author ascertained that personal perspectives on death and dying; culture; and hospice care often determine the ability of a physician to communicate effectively with patients regarding treatment options. Recommendations to bridge this gap in communication skills include a stronger emphasis in medical schools on physician-patient communication.

In chapter 4 Dr. Cynthia addressed the question, who is best to lead? By linking behavioral integrity, emotional intelligence, transformational leadership, ethics, and wisdom, she outlined a path toward ethical discipline and justice. The lessons learned focus on the responsibility of organizational leaders to be ethically responsible for their behavior and to transform the future of global organizations.

Dr. Tim broadened the view of this volume by examining the ethics related to gathering HSPII. Privacy and the maintenance of sensitive information is a critical issue in our technologically evolving world. This study focused on IT professionals and questioned the factors that support ethical behavior by individuals and organizations in this arena. A primary concern confirmed by this study was the lack of understanding by IT professionals of their ethical responsibilities.

In chapter 6, Dr. Ramon presented the results of his study that focused on the relationship of organizational culture and ethical behavior. While a leader may project the existence of an ethical culture within their organization, he or she may not understand the methodology needed to operationalize an ethical culture. From his study, Dr. Ramon concluded that a river of character runs through organizations and the moral character and emotional intelligence of the organizational leader often determined the nature of the river.

Dr. Susan considered the effect ethics and values have on leader-follower relationships in chapter 7. In her study, she assessed the impact of this relationship on team performance. The results of her study determined that better team performance was closely related to leader-follower relationships more so than to leadership style. The primary components of this relationship compared favorably to successful bottom-up change initiatives.

In chapter 8, Dr. Gail offers commentary on the power of social networking and its value to the realm of Generation F leadership. Particular emphasis was placed on common themes in communication that represent transactional and transformational leadership characteristics. The results of her study focused on the synergistic benefits of emotions, collaboration, and action using Twitter accounts.

Within chapter 9, the focus of Dr. Judy, Dr. T.G. and Dr. Cheryl was on a world without borders where globalization is the new focus of international business. These authors dig deeper, looking at the larger global community, how cultures communicate to include the importance of body language, and how this concept has affected the global landscape. Those who learn to convey their message via emotionally intelligent behavior will offer true global change.

Dr. Kaja offers insight into the world economic financial crisis with regard to debt collection in chapter 10. The purpose of her study was to determine significant differences in productivity and effectiveness of two job design models. Based on her findings, Kroll presented a debt collection model that applied the SPLM job design to enhance both collection productivity and effectiveness.

Finally, in chapter 11, Dr. Beverly looks at the wisdom of Systems Theory to provide a unique window into the psyche of an organization's mental models with regard to the advancement of women in positions of leadership. Her study critiqued organizational, social, and scientific theories of systems to assess common elements related to the models of leadership. Dr. Beverly concluded that organizations need to adopt the five disciplines described by Senge (2006) to realize the full potential of everyone in the workforce and become learning organizations.

The purpose of Volume IV of *The Refractive Thinker*(tm) was to take a journey down the path of ethics, leadership, and globalization. The collective effort of this group achieved this goal and added practical applications to this growing body of knowledge. The authors in this volume succeeded in presenting some illuminating observations on ethical leadership from significantly different perspectives that underscored the importance of ethical leadership in globalization.

As with Volume I, II, and III, Dr. Cheryl provided a refractive environment that allowed individual authors to sing their song. This was once again an enjoyable journey to the land of refractive thinking. We hope you enjoyed your exploration of ethics, leadership, and globalization, and will retain this book for future reference. See you in our next publication.

Reference

Senge, P. M. (2006). *The fifth discipline: The art & practice of the learning organization* (Revised ed.). New York: Doubleday/Currency.

Index

Other Books by the Lentz Leadership Institute

The Refractive Thinker: Volume I: An Anthology of Higher Learning

The Refractive Thinker: Volume II: Research Methodology

The Refractive Thinker: Volume III: Change Management

The Refractive Thinker: Volume IV: Ethics, Leadership, and Globalization

Coming in the Fall of 2010

The Refractive Thinker: Volume V: Research Methodology, Second Edition

MasterMinds: Graduate Anthology: Abstracts & Essays

*Available in e-book, Kindle, and individual e-chapters by author

---

Telephone orders: Call us at 877 298-5172

Fax Orders: Fax form to 877 298-5172.

Email Orders: orders@lentzleadership.com

Speaker Bookings: speakingengagements@lentzleadership.com

Website orders: Please order online via the website: http:www.lentzleadership.com. PayPal™ accepted.

Postal Orders: The Lentz Leadership Institute LLC
c/o Dr. Cheryl Lentz
9065 Big Plantation Avenue
Las Vegas, NV 89143-5440   USA

Refractive Thinker™ Press

Please send the following books:

- ☐ *The Refractive Thinker: Volume I: An Anthology of Higher Learning*
- ☐ *The Refractive Thinker: Volume II: Research Methodology*
- ☐ *The Refractive Thinker: Volume III: Change Management*
- ☐ *The Refractive Thinker: Volume IV: Ethics, Leadership, and Globalization*

Please contact the Refractive Thinker™ Press for book prices, e-book prices, and shipping.

Individual e-chapters available by author: $3.95 (plus applicable tax).
www.refractivethinker.com

Please send more FREE information:

- ☐ Speaking Engagements
- ☐ The Lentz Leadership Institute Educational Seminars
- ☐ Consulting

Join our Mailing List

Name: _____

Address: _____

City: _____ State: _____ Zip: _____

Telephone: _____ Email: _____

Sales tax: Please add 8.1% for shipping to NV addresses.

Shipping: *Please see website or contact us for exact shipping rates.*

Refractive
Thinker™
Press

Please send the following books:

- ❏ *The Refractive Thinker: Volume I: An Anthology of Higher Learning*
- ❏ *The Refractive Thinker: Volume II: Research Methodology*
- ❏ *The Refractive Thinker: Volume III: Change Management*
- ❏ *The Refractive Thinker: Volume IV: Ethics, Leadership, and Globalization*

Please contact the Refractive Thinker™ Press for book prices, e-book prices, and shipping.

Individual e-chapters available by author: $3.95 (plus applicable tax). www.refractivethinker.com

Please send more FREE information:

- ❏ Speaking Engagements
- ❏ The Lentz Leadership Institute Educational Seminars
- ❏ Consulting

Join our Mailing List

Name: _____

Address: _____

City:_____ State:_____ Zip:_____

Telephone: _____ Email: _____

Sales tax: Please add 8.1% for shipping to NV addresses.

Shipping: *Please see website or contact us for exact shipping rates.*

Refractive
Thinker™
Press

Participation in
Future Volumes of
The Refractive Thinker™

Yes I would like to participate in:

☐ **Doctoral Volume**(s) for a specific university or your organization:

    Name: _____

☐ **Graduate Volume**(s) MasterMinds for a specific university or your organization:

    Name: _____

☐ **Specialized Volume**(s) Sorority, Business, or Themed:

    Name: _____

Name:_____

Address: _____

City: _____ State: _____ Zip: _____

Telephone: _____ Email: _____

Please mail or fax form to:

The Lentz Leadership Institute LLC
c/o Dr. Cheryl Lentz
9065 Big Plantation Ave.
Las Vegas, NV 89143-5440   USA.
Fax: 877-298-5172
www.refractivethinker.com